How to Shit in the Woods

4th Edition

An Environmentally Sound Approach to a Lost Art

Kathleen Meyer

TEN SPEED PRESS
California | New York

Copyright © 1989, 1994, 2011, 2020 by Kathleen Meyer
All rights reserved.

Published in the United States by Ten Speed Press, an imprint
of Random House, a division of Penguin Random House LLC,
New York.
www.tenspeed.com

Ten Speed Press and the Ten Speed Press colophon are
registered trademarks of Penguin Random House LLC.

Library of Congress Cataloging-in-Publication Data is on file
with the publisher.

Trade Paperback ISBN: 978-1-9848-5713-2
eBook ISBN: 978-1-9848-5714-9

Printed in the United States

Illustration on page vi by Pedro Gonzalez
Chapter opening illustrations by J. S. McVey
"Poop Tube" illustration on page 66 by John Larson
Author photo by Emmalee Mueller
Design by Abhimanyu Sandal
Cover art by Sarah Weitzman

4th Printing

Fourth Edition

*In everlasting memory of the one-and-only
Jon Runnestrand.*

For my Patricio, always.

Contents

🌲

Chapter 1
Anatomy of a Crap
T. J. Crapper • Our Inhibitions • True Stories • Learning Technique •
Developing Style • Getting Comfortable • Cautions • Preserving Dignity

Chapter 2
Digging the Hole
Visualizing Worldwide Shit • Why an Environmentally Sound Hole? •
Transmission of Enteric Pathogens (Intestinal Diseases) • *Giardia:*
Symptoms, Spreading, and Roaring Debate • *Cryptosporidium* • Actual
Digging: Trowels, Soil Types, Security vs. Decomposition, and Locating the
High-Water Line • Stirring • Latrines: If You Must • Game Plan for T.P. •
What about Pee? • Ocean Disposal, or Not?

Chapter 3
When You Can't Dig a Hole
Pursuit of Unknowns • Misery Loves Company • The "Soggies" • Extreme
Adventure • Sensitive Ecosystems • High-Use Areas • Packing-It-Out: History
and Regulation • Enema Man • Group Shitarees: Discussion of Design
Features • List of Washable, Reusable Carry-Out Toilets • Do-It-Yourself Soil
Can • Rentals and Wishy-Washy Hand Washers

Chapter 4
Plight of the Solo Poop-Packer
Higher Inspiration: Junko and Jim • Becoming a Poop-Packer • Discussion
of Solo Containers • Products: Bags, Barrels, and Kits • Do-It-Yourself Poop
Tubes • Much-Needed Demise of Frosting

I dyde shyte thre grete toordes.

—Fables of Aesop, Caxton Translation, Vol. 15, 1484

Thou shalt have a place also without the camp, where thou shalt go forth abroad: And thou shalt have a paddle upon thy weapon; and it shall be when thou shalt ease thyself abroad, thou shalt dig therewith, and thou shalt turn back, and cover that which cometh from thee.

—Deuteronomy 23:12-13

Foreword

Data Point 1: The number of people heading out for hikes is growing. In the Seattle area, for instance, recent reports have the number of hikers increasing seven times faster than the population. Authorities credited (or blamed) social media! It seems hikers are 43 percent more likely to have used Instagram in the last thirty days.

Data Point 2: Increased visitation leads to sanitation problems. In the High Peaks of the Adirondacks, for instance, "staff come upon people in the midst of pooping on the trails," says Julia Goren, education director for the local mountain club. Officials were defining it (nonironically, apparently) as "the number one stewardship issue" for the biggest state park in the country.

Data Point 3: When official systems dealing with human waste evaporate for even a few days—say, when the president of the United States throws a tantrum and closes the government—chaos reigns: the government shutdown at the start of 2019 resulted in myriad reports of the composting toilets in national parks overflowing. "Appalling," one official put it.

All of which is to say, thank heaven that Kathleen Meyer's publisher is sending her classic out into the world again. It provides the same great service it did upon its original publication in 1989 (back in the days when the title was actually kind of shocking). The learning curve for us is easy—this is not like studying to play the violin or speak Mandarin. We emerge from it better, more resourceful, people more able to deal with the modern vicissitudes of life.

Read it as a guide but also as a metaphor. I published a book in 1989 too, *The End of Nature*, which was the first book for a general audience about global warming or, as we called it then, "the greenhouse effect." In the intervening few decades, we have endlessly poured more carbon into the atmosphere, heating the earth. We have, as it were, a big waste problem. We're turning the planet into a dump—as Pope Francis put it in his remarkable encyclical *Laudato Si,* "The earth, our home, is beginning to look more and more like an immense pile of filth."

So when you're squatting in the bushes, too busy to sneak a peek at Twitter, take the moment to consider how what you're learning in these pages might, in parallel, apply to the even greater problems that threaten our lovely home. This volume is immensely practical, in deep and powerful ways.

—**Bill McKibben**, author of *Falter: Has the Human Game Begun to Play Itself Out?* and cofounder of 350.org

Preface

In response to Nature's varied calls, *How to Shit in the Woods* presents a collection of techniques (stumbled upon by the author, usually in a most graceless fashion) to assist the latest generation of backwoods enthusiasts still fumbling with their drawers. Just as important is the intention to answer a different and more desperate cry, from Nature herself, by conveying essential, explicit environmental precautions about wilderness toilet habits—applicable to a variety of seasons and climates and terrains.

For many millennia our ancestors successfully squatted in the woods. You might think it would come by instinct, nature simply taking its course when a colon is bulging or a bladder bursting. But "its course," I cheerlessly and laboriously discovered, is subject to infinite disastrous destinations.

Years of guiding city folks down whitewater rivers sharpened my squatting skills and assured me I wasn't alone in the klutz department. Frequently, the strife and anxiety experienced in the bushes were more intense than any sweat produced by the downstream roar of a monster, raft-eating rapid. Those river days led me to a couple of firm conclusions. One: Monster rapids inspire a lot of squatting, which in turn supports a wealth of study material for two. Two (ultimately one of the subjects that prompted this publication): Finesse at shitting in the woods—or anywhere else outdoors—is not come by instinctively. That might sound as though I were a regular Peeping Joan. But with several dozen bodies squatting behind the few bushes and boulders of a narrow river canyon, I found it practically impossible not to trip over a few—exhibiting all manner of contorted expressions and positions—every day. Generally, a city-bred adult can expect to be no more successful than a tottering one-year-old in dropping his or her pants to squat. Shitting in the woods is an acquired rather than innate skill, a skill honed only by practice, a skill all but lost to the bulk of the population along with the art of making soap, carding wool, and skinning buffalo.

We are now many generations potty-trained on indoor plumbing and accustomed to our privacy, comfort, and convenience. To a person raised with a spiffy, silenced, flush toilet, sequestered behind a bolted bathroom door, having to go in the backcountry can rapidly degenerate into a frightening physical hazard, an embarrassing mess, or, incredibly, a weeklong attack of avoidance constipation.

A lust for wilderness vacations and exotic treks keeps exploding out of our metropolitan confines. As victims of urban madness, we fervently seek respite in the wilds. Masses of bodies thunder through forests, scurry up mountain peaks, flail down rivers, and, without serious attention on our part, leave a wake of toilet paper and fecal matter that Mother Nature cannot fathom. It's not unrealistic to fear that within a few more years the last remaining pristine places could well exhibit conditions equal to the world's worst slums.

Anyone who has come upon a favorite, once-lovely beach, camp, or mountain lake trashed by the likes of soiled toilet paper, baby diapers, and raw turds understands the horror. But greater than the visual impact of human toilet trash are the veiled environmental consequences. No longer can we drink from even the most remote, crystal clear streams without the possibility of contracting diseases.

And once the "authorities" step in and take over preservation, it is, to my mind, already too late. Rules and regulations imposed by government agencies (now absolutely necessary in many areas) can themselves be rude incursions on majestically primitive surroundings and antipodal to the freedom wildness represents. Rules, signs, application forms, and their ensuing costs are truly a pain in the ass, brought about not solely by increased numbers of people, but also by the innocently unaware and the blatantly irresponsible. It is to these sacred, wild havens that we journey to heal and revitalize. We cherish what they deliver in high challenge, copious physical sweating, magnificent exhilaration, and the divine gifts of quietude and profound wonder. With our lives under incessant assault from modern-day stresses and crises—from just plain existing to all out planet-saving—the stakes for caretaking our wildlands turn evermore crucial. A willingness to *inspire* preservation comes most naturally from those who delight in the untrammeled wilds; it is they—we—who have the greatest responsibility to generate respect, care, and education. It is we who must learn and teach others how and where to shit in the woods.

Author's Note

When long ago I set about scribbling this book's first chapter, everyone but for a few friends counseled that "shit" would be no word for a cover, no word for a bookstore window—I should title it *When Nature Calls*. "Too blah," I'd muttered. "Too esoteric." Driven, as I was, by sights of desecrated beaches and woodland trails, the voice that kept bubbling up from within was one of directness. My mission, as I saw it, was to haul this taboo topic into the light of day. One seemingly insurmountable problem stood in my way: terminology. How was I to refer to this stuff that is pushed and squirted out of bodies in response to eating and drinking?

Shit and *pee*. Running through all the alternatives produced no sensible solutions. Studding an entire book with *urination, defecation, elimination,* and *stools* seemed depressingly clinical. The pronunciation alone of the terms *bowel movement* and *BM* emitted something foul—from my childhood, I remembered them being breathed in whispers. *Bathroom* and *restroom* are euphemisms not applicable in the woods; even *outhouse* and *Porta Potti* do not fit where they do not exist. *Scats, turds, dung, chips, pellets,* and *pies* are useful mainly in zoology and dirty jokes. *Constitutional* sounded overly prissy in addition to misleading; I had never heard of anything but a "morning constitutional," easily confused with a brisk turn in the fresh air. *John, johnny, head, potty, wee-wee, pee-pee, whizz, number one* and *number two, tinkle, poop, load, poo-poo, doo-doo, ca-ca,* and "going to see a man about a horse"—all a little too cutesy or indirect.

Next I tried circumventing the problem by relying on description and avoiding particular terms altogether, but the prose became lengthy and cumbersome; plus, I'd be accused of not calling a crap a crap. Stuck again, not another noun in sight.

My mind wandered back through the tangle of verbiage, in search of a new trail, something missed. I remembered that my father had always purported to be within his genteel rights in using the word *piss*, because Shakespeare had employed it. Father's strategy seemed excellent (though he was technically wrong; it was Jonathan Swift), and over the years my refined (verging on priggish) mother did grow, if reluctantly, to accept this argument. Although she never came to use the word herself, in time the wince that wrinkled up her face upon its utterance became almost indiscernible. Thus, with a solid case in point and Mother's brief but significant evolution in mind, a defensible logic began to take hold.

The printed word has a way of inventing truths (as the success of several sleazy national tabloids and "fake news" attest) and influencing acceptable usage, with *Webster's* dictionary being considered a most reliable reference. Excitement seized me as I noted that although my 1957 unabridged edition of *Webster's* contained no mention of *shit*, the library's 1988 edition *did* include the term, plus a three-line definition. Aha! What do you know? Linguistic history in the making.

Subsequently, I remembered something E. B. White had written about language that had stuck in my head, no doubt, because of his choice in metaphor—rivers being close to my heart:

> *The language is perpetually in flux: It is a living stream, shifting, changing, receiving new strength from a thousand tributaries, losing old forms in the backwaters of time.*

Shit hadn't been lost in any backwater. White, had he still been alive, might well have been horrified by my using his explanation for my justification, but, unwittingly and to my immense joy, I found he supplied more and more defense for my crystallizing rationale:

> *A new word is always up for survival. Many do survive. Others grow stale and disappear. Most are, at least in their infancy, more appropriate to conversation than to composition.*

By no means had *shit* grown stale. For hundreds of years, *shit* had survived with ease. I knew it to be an old word: *scitan* in Old English and *shyte* in Middle English. In modern times, *shit* abounded in daily conversation. With *Webster's* branding its usage as "vulgar," I concluded the word was lolling in its infancy.

With the needed precedent set, I fell right into keeping with Father's old strategy. My lacking the literary stature of a Shakespeare or Swift became no matter. Feeling as exuberant as one of E. B. White's thousand burbling tributaries, I proposed to help wash this great word, *shit*, downstream to its confluence with greater maturity and on into the ocean of acceptable usage. There it might float around in the company of all other words deemed proper for composition. And so it was that I settled in earnest on the promotion of *shit*, and *pee* along with it, accompanied by splashes of the clinical and cutesy in appropriate places.

Shit is a superb word, really. *Shit* can be music to my ears. It need not be spoken in hushed, moralizing tones. "SHIT! OH, SHEEIT!" Versatile and articulate, it's indeed a pleasure to shout, to keen through one's teeth. A perfectly audible—if not ear-shattering—remarkably ordinary, decent, modest, everyday word.

Furthermore, it became my thought that in legitimately defining *shit* I might engender some small credibility for the word with anyone still shocked by its usage. For the too well-bred and the overly delicate, for the betterment of the English language, and perhaps for the next edition of *Webster's*, I offer at the end of the text a complete, unabridged definition of *shit*. For all its subtleties of meaning, this word is extremely unambiguous. *Shit*, in fact, is one of the least misunderstood words in use today.

As it turned out, when finally in print, my guide in all its shitty glory shot out the gate at the Frankfurt Book Fair, running away with the 1989 *Bookseller* magazine's prize for "Oddest Book Title of the Year," and the next thing I knew—well, nearly—it had become a training aid for the respectable likes of scout troops, outdoor schools, wilderness programs for inner-city youth, and Bible camps; for rangers with the US Forest Service, National Park Service, and Bureau of Land Management; for whitewater rafting guides; and for members of the military. Word filtered back that copies had been spotted gracing a library shelf at McMurdo Station, Antarctica; selling in a country store north of the Arctic Circle; a bookstore in South Africa; a B&B in Scotland. Tickling me the most—in the *window* of Artist's Proof, my favorite local bookstore, there it sat!

Today, our sensibilities about toilet practices have noticeably ascended to new and breezier heights, with titters and embarrassment clearly on the decline. *Shit* is less of a societal shock, with the internet being a different kind of beast. The 2019 Merriam-Webster Online Dictionary provides four parts of speech (noun, intransitive

and transitive verb, adjective, interjection), a number of defini-
tions, recordings of four pronunciations, and a history from the
fourteenth century. Progress! Still, the word remains forbidden on
the airwaves, until we reach civilized Canada.

The one dubious legacy of this guide is its having spawned a
rash of other *shit*-titled books. Yet I indeed hope it influenced—at
least in part—the leaping of bodily eliminations onto the plain of
charming children's books. Two of my favorites: *Everyone Poops* by
Taro Gomi; and, adorable, *The Story of the Little Mole Who Went in
Search of Whodunit* [Who, pray tell, pooped on his head?] by Werner
Holzwarth and Wolf Erlbruch . . . as here is where all successful
campaigns must begin, with youngsters. Nonetheless, some few
centuries might be needed before the word *shit* loses its firecracker
appeal to kids. I relate the following story:

> Once upon a time, a woman named Tia, a farrier by
> profession, sat on her commode reading a few pages
> of the first edition of this book—in fact, the very pages
> preceding this one. In turning over in her mind my
> theories on the evolution of the word shit, she came
> upon the notion of imparting to her children a new
> attitude toward the sound of s-h-i-t. Their generation
> might then, she thought, grow up in plain acceptance
> of the word, reacting to it as they might now to "puppy"
> or "bubble gum." At that moment, her seven-year-old
> son appeared at the bathroom door asking if she
> would accompany him to the trampoline. On impulse,
> she said, "Just as soon as Mama's through shitting."
>
> SHITTING? MAMA'S SHITTING? His eyes grew round as
> his trampoline. Out to the yard he ran, broadcasting
> to his brother and inadvertently the whole neighbor-
> hood: "MAMA'S SHITTING!!!"

It's quite possible that we could coordinate my farrier friend's
effort at advancing etymology by synchronizing a time around the
globe to tell all seven-year-olds about shitting. Then we can all
stand aghast together while our offspring shout to the neighbors.
The whole thing should be over in a week.

1
Anatomy of a Crap

Bowels are not exactly a polite subject for conversation, but they are certainly a common problem. . . . Please think of me again as the urologist's daughter. . . . It may disgust you that I have brought it up at all, but who knows? Life has some problems which are basic for all of us—and about which we have a natural reticence.

—Katharine Hepburn, *The Making of the African Queen*

In the mid-1800s, in the Royal Borough of Chelsea, London, an industrious young English plumber named Thomas Crapper grabbed progress in his pipe wrench and with a number of sophisticated sanitation inventions leapfrogged ahead one hundred years. T. J. Crapper found himself challenged by problems we wrestle with yet today: water quality and water conservation. Faced with London's diminishing reservoirs, drained almost dry by the valve leakage and "continuous flush systems" of early water closets, Crapper developed the *water waste preventer*—the very siphonic cistern with uphill flow and automatic shut-off found in modern toilet tanks. T. Crapper & Co Ld, Sanitary Engineers, Marlboro Works, Chelsea (as his name still appears on three manhole covers in Westminster Abbey) was also responsible for the laying of hundreds of miles of London's connecting sewers—and none too soon. The River Thames carried such quantities of rotting turds that the

1

effluvium had driven Parliament to convene in the early morning hours to avoid a vile off-river breeze.

For the Victorian ladies who complained of the WC's hissing and gurgling as giving away their elaborately disguised trips to the loo, Crapper installed the first silencers. Such pretenses as "pricking the plum pudding" or "picking the daisies" were foiled when a lady's absence was accompanied by crashing waterfalls and echoing burbles. Among Mr. Crapper's other claims to fame were his pear-shaped toilet seat (the forerunner of the gap-front seat), designed for men, and the posthumous addition to the English language of a vibrant new word: *crapper!*

Clearly, T. J. Crapper was ahead of his day. Progress and time, nonetheless, are peculiar concepts. Some things in the universe—to name a few: pollution, the use of euphemisms, *sneaking* off to the bathroom to tinkle silently down the side of the bowl—seem to defy change, even from century to century. But there's been one glaring reversal in regard to crap. Our twenty-first-century populace, well advanced beyond the novelties and quirks of the first indoor WCs, finds itself having to break entirely new ground, as it were, when relieving itself outdoors. Ironically, shitting in the woods successfully—that is, without adverse environmental, psychological, or physical consequences—might be deemed genuine progress today. Take Henry, for instance (a namesake, perhaps, or even a descendant of old King Henry VIII).

> All the stories you are about to read are true (for the most part), having been extracted from dear friends and voluble strangers on various occasions, sometimes following the ingestion of copious quantities of Jose Cuervo or Yukon Jack. Only the names have been changed to protect the incommodious.

High on a dusty escarpment jutting skyward from camp, a man named Henry, having scrambled up there and squeezed in behind what appeared to be the ideal bush for camouflage, began lowering himself precariously into a deep knee bend. Far below, just out of their bedrolls, three fellow river runners violated the profound quiet of canyon's first light by poking about the commissary, cracking eggs, snapping twigs, and sloshing out the coffee pot. Through the branches, our pretzel man on the hill observed the breakfast preparations while proceeding with his own morning mission. To the earth it finally fell, round and firm, this sturdy turd. With a bit more encouragement from gravity, it rolled slowly out from between Henry's big boots, threaded its way through the spindly trunks of the "ideal" bush, and then, truly taking on a mind of its own, leaped into the air like a downhill skier out at the gate.

You can see the dust trail of a fast-moving pickup mushrooming off a dirt road long after you've lost sight of the truck. Henry watched, wide-eyed and helpless, as a similar if smaller cloud billowed up defiantly below him, and the actual item became obscured from view. Zigging and zagging, it caromed off rough spots in the terrain. Madly it bumped and tumbled and dropped, as if making its run through a giant pinball machine. Gaining momentum, gathering its own little avalanche, round and down it spun like a buried back tire spraying up sand. All too fast it raced down the steep slope—until becoming locked in that deadly slow motion common to the fleeting seconds just preceding all imminent, unalterable disasters. With one last bounce, one final effort at heavenward orbit, this unruly goofball (followed by an arcing tail of debris) landed in a terminal thud and a rain of pebbly clatter not six inches from the bare foot of the woman measuring out coffee.

With his dignity thus unraveled along sixty yards of descent, Henry in all likelihood might have come home from his first river trip firmly resolved to never again set foot past the end of the asphalt. Of course, left to his own devices and with any determination at all unless he was a total fumble-bum, Henry would have learned how to shit in the woods. Eventually. The refining of his skills by trial and error and the acquiring of grace, poise, and self-confidence—not to mention muscle development and balance—would probably have taken him about as long as it did me: years.

I don't think Henry would mind our taking a closer look at his calamity. Henry can teach us a lot, and not all by poor example. Indeed, he started out on the right track by getting far enough away from camp to ensure his privacy. Straight up just wasn't the best choice of direction. Next, he chose a location with a view, although whether he took time to appreciate it is unknown. Usually I recommend a wide-reaching view, a landscape rolling away to distant mountain peaks and broad expanses of wild sky. But a close-in setting near a lichen-covered rock, a single wildflower, or even dried-up weeds and monotonous talus, when quietly studied, can offer inspiration of a different brand.

The more time you spend in the wild, the easier it will be to reconnoiter an inspiring view. A friend of mine calls her morning exercise the *Advanced Wilderness Appreciation Walk*. As she strides along an irrigation canal practically devoid of vegetation, but overgrown with crumpled beer cans, has-been appliances, and rusted auto parts, she finds the morning's joy in the colors of the sunrise and the backlighting of a lone thistle.

Essential for the outdoor neophyte is a breathtaking view. Such opportunities for glorious moments alone in the presence of grandeur should be soaked up. They are soul-replenishing and mind-expanding. The ideal occasion for communing with nature is while you're peacefully sitting still—yes, shitting in the woods. The rest of the day, unless you're trekking solo, can quickly become cluttered with social or organizational distractions.

But back to Henry, whose only major mistake was failing to dig a hole. It's something to think about: a small hole preventing the complete destruction of an ego. A proper hole is of great importance, not only in averting disasters such as Henry's, but also in preventing the spread of disease and facilitating rapid decomposition. Chapter 2 in its entirety is devoted to the hole.

More dos and don'ts for preserving physical and mental health while shitting in the woods will become apparent as we look in on Charles. He has his own notion about clothes and pooping in the wilderness: he takes them off. Needless to say, this man hikes well away from camp and any connecting trails to a place where he feels secure about completely removing his britches and relaxing for a spell. Finding an ant-free log, he digs his hole on the opposite side from the view, sits down, scoots to the back of the log, and floats into the rhapsody that tall treetops find among the clouds. Remember this one. It's by far the dreamiest, most relaxing setup for shitting in the woods. No agonizing stress for our squatting and balance muscles. A smooth rock (or even a backpack in a pinch in a vacant expanse) can be used in the same manner—for hanging your buns over the back.

This seems like an appropriate spot to share a helpful technique imparted to me one day by another friend: "Shit first, dig later." In puzzlement, I turned to her and as our eyes met she watched mine grow into harvest moons. But of course, "shit first, dig later"—that way, you would never miss the hole. It was the perfect solution! Perfect, that is, for anyone with bad aim. Me? Not me.

Unlike Charles, there's my longtime friend Elizabeth who prizes the usefulness of her clothes. While on a rattletrap bus trip through northern Mexico, the lumbering vehicle on which she rode came to a five-minute halt in compensation for the lack of a toilet on board. Like a colorful parachute descending from desert skies, Lizzie's voluminous skirt billowed to the earth, and she squatted down inside her own private outhouse.

Occasionally it is impossible to obtain an optimal degree of privacy. Some years back, my colleague Ali was hitchhiking along the Autobahn in Germany, where the terrain was board flat and barren. At last, unable to contain herself, she asked the driver to stop and she struck out across a field toward a knoll topped by a lone bush. There, hidden by branches and feeling safe from the eyes of traffic, she squatted and swung up the back of her skirt, securing it as a cape over her head. Then Ali's rejoicing abruptly ended. Out of nowhere came a column of Boy Guides (the rear guard?) marching past her bare derrière. There's something to be said here for the parachute approach.

Another version of Ali's story needs to be kept in mind when hiking switchbacks. I was once pounding up a mountain when the trail took a looping turn and the strong stench of bear blew in my face. Peering left, peering right, I saw nothing. *She must have loped across here and skedaddled.* But the fright had set off more than my nerves. I was soon well off the path, shrouded by low-hanging branches, a soft mullein leaf in hand, and, having excavated a nice hole with my trowel, settled into a full squat, when smack at me came three hikers, all men, stepping smartly along. Compass bearings kaput, I'd tacked straight across the dogleg to within ten feet of the lower path. It was only the trail's ruts and roots, which held the hikers' attention, and my holding my breath like a startled squirrel that saved me. Advice? Keep extra brains about you on switchback routes, not to mention bear country.

There are dozens of theories on clothes and shitting, all individual and personal. In time you will develop your own. Edwin, our next case study, hatched a new approach to clothes after one memorable hunting trip; whether it be to take them off or keep them on, I haven't figured out.

For the better part of a nippy fall morning, Edwin had been slinking through mountain ranges of gnarly underbrush in pursuit of an elusive six-pointer. Trudging relentlessly along with no luck, he finally became discouraged, a cold drizzle adding to his gloom. At last, a lovely meadow opened before him, its beauty causing him to pause. His attention averted from the deer, he now relaxed into a gaze of pleasure, and then shortly became aware of his physical discomforts: every weary muscle, every labored joint, every miniscule bramble scratch—and then another pressing matter.

Coming upon a log beneath a spreading tree, Edwin propped up his rifle, quickly slipped off his poncho, and slid the suspenders from his shoulders. Whistling now, he sat and he shat. But when he turned to bid it farewell, not a thing was there *there*. Oh, hell! In total disbelief, Edwin peered over the log once more, still finding nothing. The sky opened and it began to rain and a pleasant vision of camp beckoned. Preparing to leave, he yanked on his poncho and hefted his gun. To warm his ears, he pulled up his hood. There, oh *there* it was! On top of his head, melting in the rain like a scoop of ice cream left in the sun.

Poor Edwin will not soon forget this day; he walked seven miles before coming across enough water to clean up. Though I fear he was in no humor to be thinking much beyond himself, we can only hope he didn't wash directly in the stream. To keep pollutants from entering the waterways, it's important to use a bucket to haul wash water well above the high-water line of spring runoff. But I digress, and this topic is covered thoroughly in the next chapter.

When he was eighty-six years old, my dear Uncle Ernie was cautioning old people fearful of toppling over while squatting (old people?) to steady themselves by holding on to a branch or a tree trunk. It's lately come to my attention that Uncle Ernie's tactic requires an added warning. Sergio Jauregui, longtime Baja guide and owner of Todos Santos Eco Adventures, related an episode collected from one of his hiking clients. We'll call her Susie Falls Down Squish. Sergio came by this rather personal story because Susie, after saying she'd be "right back," apparently felt the need to explain her great tardiness upon returning to camp. She had trotted off on a mission of evacuation. While in a squat, she'd sought to steady herself by grabbing ahold of a branch. The branch snapped! "What might have taken her ten minutes," Sergio said, with a sympathetic wince, "stretched into an hour." Hence, should Uncle Ernie's approach be one that appeals to you, be sure to select a strong and living branch on a species that is not brittle—or, you, like Susie, could land precisely in the spot you'd rather not. My theory is to find a place to sit: I'm actually Charles in disguise, the sitting dreamer.

If you're a good squatter and also in a hurry, perhaps to chase a caribou or click off pictures of the sunset, you might try a technique perfected by one of our elected US officials. We'll call him Jonathan the Ungulate Hunter, and, I might add, the Ham. His is a rare performance, an adagio of fluid motion and perfect balance. One night after midnight, at the tail end of a venison barbecue bash, I mentioned I was writing this book and received a narrated mock demonstration on the living room rug.

Sinking into a hang-ten surfboard pose—knees bent and arms outstretched from the shoulders—Jonathan scrapes a trench four to five inches deep with the heel of one cowboy boot. "This works," he says, "only where the earth is soft." Addressing those of us still in the room, he suggests dropping your jeans (and drops his) either to just below your hips or all the way to your ankles, pointing out that folds of material are uncomfortable when bunched up in the bends at the back of your knees. After squat-straddling the ditch for as long as it takes, he drops in his paper and shoves the excavated dirt back into the trough with the instep of his boot. As a finale, he packs down the dirt the way any good gardener would finish planting a tree. It was a marvelous performance, I had to agree, except for the toilet paper in the hole—the telltale sign of humans on the planet. We'll discuss this later.

From the depths of many a lumpy sleeping bag, from the middle of many a wilderness campsite, comes this sort of question accompanied by a bit of a whine: "Herb? Whaddo I do if I have to go in the middle of the night?" Secretly, Herb might harbor an identical first-time question, so I'll answer this one for him.

Unless there's a full moon or you have the nocturnal instincts of the snails that go for my petunias, carry a flashlight for those midnight jaunts. As much as I dislike anything resembling civilization in the boondocks, I will concede that in unfamiliar terrain, a tiny lightbulb can prevent a stubbed toe, a cracked head—when you trip and pitch over the cliff—or, more commonly, two weeks of itchy crotch-crazies from lurking poison oak. Many contributors to this book have confessed to one of those I-hoped-I-wouldn't-live-long-enough-to-tell-the-story stories. Poison oak (or ivy or sumac) seems to be the most common misadventure of night squatting.

One further warning: make it a *small* flashlight. The searchlight variety is overkill and can predispose the body to more permanent damage from irate fellow campers. There's nothing like waking up in the middle of peaceful nowhere to someone crashing through the bushes with her high beam and a roll of toilet paper.

Observant caution is always the recommended approach in selecting a place to relieve oneself. Poison oak is not the only dastardly culprit abroad. As my friend Ma Prudence Barker notes, one cannot just plop down with wild abandon in any old daisy field—especially a daisy field—and hope to escape unscathed. Ma once knew a logger named Lloyd who experienced the unequivocal misery of being nailed by a bumblebee smack on the family jewels. Logger Lloyd swore the pain was worse than any chainsaw nick, bullet hole, or careless imprint of boot caulks tearing into flesh.

It's prudent to inspect any area for hazards where you plan to sit down bare-assed. You wouldn't want to become an outdoor casualty, as did the subject of this poem by Shirley Vogler Meister.

The Ex-Camper

Though city-bred, he learned to camp
and loved to trek in dew and damp
until a creeping critter found
him crouching with his denims down.

My own stinging affair transpired on a late-afternoon saunter along the ever-captivating Bitterroot River, near my home. Half a mile downstream from the fishing access, I began to hear nature's call, and it grew rapidly into a booming holler. "You can always skip a meal," a friend once said, "but when you gotta go, you gotta go!" I beelined across the cobblestone beach, up the embankment, and into the woodlands. Immediately—and fortuitously, I thought at the time—I came upon an area of deadfall that presented several downed trees and quickly selected a handy one, smooth-trunked, requiring only the tossing aside of an overlaying branch. As I was unbuttoning my cargo pants and stripping down the straps of my one-piece bathing suit, a buzzing that didn't register as threatening trained my eyes to a slab of bark canted over the grasses at my feet. *Oh, yuck! Someone's been here and done their doody!* I was just envisioning a pack of intently busy flies, when—Yeow! Nailed! On the shoulder, the underarm, the back. Swinging wildly at the attack, I ran, stumbling, screaming back to the beach. (Ground-nesting yellow jackets are among the fiercest of hornets.) In retrospect, I can't believe I didn't spontaneously water my pants. The urge, in fact, completely shut down until my strolling partner had removed fourteen stingers from welts the size of fifty-cent-pieces and I was again home.

Is there a moral to this story? Well, for me, there is: keep on teaching outdoor toilet etiquette, in order to better trust that other river walkers won't be leaving messy piles under hunks of bark. And then, at first sign of buzzing, RUN LIKE CRAZY.

Also stay alert for the presence of other critters. Snakes are notorious for snoozing tucked under rocks and logs. Ants run around everywhere. And there are places in the world, as the noted writer and explorer Tim Cahill discovered, where a person can't squat (to shit) without carrying a big stick to beat off the local pigs. Always check around for damage you might incur. And check for damage you might inflict.

One morning on the Owyhee River in Oregon, our party had already broken camp, loaded the boats, and tied down everything securely. We were standing ready to push off into the current when it became apparent to me that the morning's coffee had arrived at the end of its course through my innards.

"Wait, wait," I cried to everyone and raced up the bank, winding through the jumble of boulders until a convenient rock presented itself. Yanking down my shorts, I sat down and began to water the face of the rock.

Now the southeastern corner of Oregon is home to the chukar, a relative of the partridge. This chunky, chickenlike bird is saddled with a reputation for being absurdly stupid and has the added hereditary misfortune of a lunatic voice. A cuckoo bird with the hiccups couldn't sound sillier. Audubon calls the chukar a "hardy game bird that can outrun a hunter (first flying uphill, then flying down)." It's been my experience that if you were to decide on chukar for dinner, you could walk right up to one, hand it a stone, and it would agreeably hit itself over the head for you. Combine the bird's inability for anything resembling graceful flight with its darting, quick-stepping motion reminiscent of an old-time movie, add long hours spent ridiculously burping its own name, and the chukar becomes cause for much amusement.

Still propped on the rock, I was appreciating a final glance around one of my favorite river camps while enjoying the pleasure of a shrinking bladder. Suddenly, there came a loud, crazed *chukkarr chuk-karr*. A great flapping motion arose from between my knees, convulsed into my face, and then vanished. I knelt down before the wet rock. Tucked beneath a small overhang, behind a clump of grass, I discovered a precious woven nest holding eight warm eggs—now lakefront property on the edge of a puddle of piss. In one great swoop of karma, all my abusive snickering and pompous guffawing, my enjoyment at the expense of this poor species of fowl had come home to roost and I felt terrible. Atop a nearby boulder after her fit of apoplexy, the ruffled mother sat staring at me. While heading back to the beach, I chided the powers that be for not giving me a more acute sense of smell or hearing—in the absence of experience—and resolved to do more vigorous battle with my ignorance.

(Recently, inadvertently, I unearthed some added facts about chukars. They are an "introduced" species—boo!—who eat cheatgrass—yay! Chukar farms have existed since 1921. You can order eggs and hatch your own. They are said to "make wonderful indoor pets" that are extremely loyal. Who knew!)

Most of the foregoing stories are worst-case scenarios. I have recounted them not to scare you out of the woods, but to acknowledge real perils and suggest how to work around them. Life itself is a risk; you could trip headlong over your own big toe or swallow your breakfast down the wrong pipe any day of the week.

Should you be a person who—out of sheer dread of the "complete wilderness experience"—tends to remain longingly planted at the edge of the forest others are hiking, or moored to the bank of the river others are floating, I urge you, instead, to summon your pluck. Find a place of privacy, a "place of easement" as the Elizabethans knew it. Find a panoramic view. And go for it! Then, ascend to a sage of squatting . . . READ ON.

2
Digging the Hole

Landscape is sacramental, to be read as text.
—Seamus Heaney, *Preoccupations*

When we try to pick something by itself, we find it hitched to everything else in the universe.
—John Muir, *Daily Journal*, 1869

Now for the serious stuff. People—corporate CEOs, Wall Street barons, philandering spouses, public officials, lofty presidents—always want to know how to bury their shit. This chapter spells out precisely where and how to dig holes that promote rapid decomposition of feces and prevent contamination of waterways, thereby providing the best protection for the health of humans, the rest of the animal kingdom, and the planet. Before we can hope to fathom how great is the importance of properly digging our own small one-sit hole (also termed *cat hole*) in the bush, it's necessary to try to envision our shit in the global sense. *Try* is the trick here.

Exactly where does the world's collective excrement go? Not a pleasant question. How often do any of us ponder where it goes after it's sucked down the hole in the bottom of the bowl? Possibly never. Such reflections tend to detour our consciousness, barring those rare occasions when we have to call Roto-Rooter.

Approached from any angle, the actual physical dimensions of this pile of crap produced upon our globe befuddle imagining.

Nevertheless, let's go back to the Mesozoic era and try thinking across the ages—across mountain ranges, across continents—to the present. Let's begin with dinosaur scats.

In all probability, the *Stegosaurus* and *Tyrannosaurus rex* let rip with something the size of a HUMMER. The piles left by the woolly mammoth might have been somewhat smaller, say, Mini Cooper–size—nonetheless, a formidable turd. To the total of the dinosaurs' leavings add the excrement of Cro-Magnon man (and woman) and the wandering tribes. Add the feces of polar bears, black bears, brown bears, gorillas, hippos, and giraffes. Add buffalo chips. Add tiger and rhino dung. Tally up the dumps of the Romans (remembering their gluttonous ways), the Vikings (that stout-of-digestion breed), and modern man, woman, and infant (by all means infant—we know how the human baby goes at it). Include the scats of elephant and lion, deer and antelope, moose and kangaroo, caribou and wallaby. Toss in every species that birdshits—from pterodactyl to parakeet. Round up the output of hogs, dogs, horses, cows, rabbits, owls, cats, and rats. And in imagining all this, you'll have put a mere chicken scratch on the surface.

Anyone who's been responsible for the maintenance of a cat's litter box understands how turds have the inherent tendency to pile up like junk mail. And anyone who's ever skipped across a cow pasture has devoted at least a few seconds to marveling at the size of those rippled pies (if not sailing the dried ones like Frisbees). Now, multiply one—just one—litter box or cow by 230 million years. Gadzooks!

Since the minutest scrap of life began wriggling around on our planet, Mother Earth has been valiantly embracing fecal waste in an astounding display of her natural absorption capacities. An infinitely bottomless garbage pit, however, does not exist. There are times when the amount of waste becomes far too great for it to be amassed comfortably against her bosom. And the amount of waste can often have less to do with the problem than the manner in which we discard it.

Take, for instance, all the campers in Yellowstone National Park on one good-weather weekend and imagine them as a herd of buffalo corralled in a space the size of your backyard. Or take all the voyagers on a cruise ship and visualize them housed for a month inside your local movie theater, minus plumbing. In the absence of adequate facilities, accumulated fecal matter rapidly grows into a major sanitation problem, sometimes with devastating consequences. Under such conditions, diseases find king-size footholds from which to run rampant. Epidemics—not to mention assaults on the aesthetics—are common in regions where the tonnage of yuck exceeds absorption capacities. Fecally transmitted diseases are endemic in most developing countries, but they are not unheard of in the United States.

Until roughly the mid-1970s, no one ever considered it unsafe to drink directly from mountain streams. You could stretch out on the bank of a high mountain meadow creek and just push your face into the water to drink. In 1977, the Sierra Club backpacker's guide still touted drinking directly from wilderness waterways as one of the "very special pleasures" of backcountry travel. In 1968, Edward Abbey wrote the following in *Desert Solitaire* (New York: Ballantine, 1985):

> When late in the afternoon I finally stumbled—sun-dazed, blear-eyed, parched as an old bacon rind—upon that blue stream which flows like a miraculous mirage down the floor of the canyon, I was too exhausted to pause and drink soberly from the bank. Dreamily, deliriously, I waded into the waist-deep water and fell on my face. Like a sponge I soaked up moisture through every pore, letting the current bear me along beneath a canopy of overhanging willow trees. I had no fear of drowning in the water—I intended to drink it all.

But no longer can we "drink it all"—no longer can we drink even a drop before disinfecting it, without running the risk of getting sick. According to the Centers for Disease Control and Prevention (CDC) in Atlanta, no surface water in the world is guaranteed free of the microscopic cysts responsible for a parasitic disease called giardiasis. This is a disease not easily eradicated—in the wilds, nor sometimes in the human body. Although not fatal in healthy adults, it can be an unpleasant and debilitating illness and, in some cases, chronic. For the very young, the old, or the frail, it can be worse. It is curiously also possible to be asymptomatic: carry the disease but show no symptoms. In the medical community in some locations, giardiasis is still an obscure disease and the general public can be instrumental in promoting an awareness of it. To that end, I've reprinted here a list of specific symptoms.

Symptoms of Giardiasis (Commonly Called *Giardia*)

1. Sudden onset of explosive diarrhea seven to ten days after ingestion, especially in conjunction with wilderness or foreign travel (other sources to consider are dogs, cats, and preschool daycare centers).
2. A large volume of foul-smelling, loose (but not watery) stools, accompanied by abdominal distention, flatulence, and cramping.
3. Nausea, vomiting, lack of appetite, headache, and low fever.
4. Acute symptoms can last seven to twenty-one days, and can become chronically persistent or relapsing.
5. In chronic cases, significant weight loss can occur due to malabsorption of nutrients.
6. In chronic cases, bulky, loose, foul-smelling stools—or greasy, light-colored stools that tend to float—can persist or recur.
7. Chronic symptoms include flatulence, bloating, constipation, and upper abdominal cramps.

(Although it's thought that most cases resolve spontaneously within four to six weeks, if you think you have *Giardia*, you should see your health care provider for stool testing and medication. With any diarrhea illness, replenishing body fluids is critical. Keep in mind that the symptoms given above are nonspecific; many other problems can exhibit the same symptoms. In fact, when testing stool samples nowadays, it is recommended to test for both *Giardia* and another protozoan prolific in surface waters, *Cryptosporidium*, discussed later in this chapter.)

The Great *Giardia* Debate

The actual spread of the *Giardia lamblia* parasite into the backcountry is an interesting and, as of yet, incomplete story. Although the particulars of transmission are still under study, it has been determined that strains can be passed between animals and humans. Like many of the world's enteric pathogens (intestinal bugs), *Giardia* is spread by "fecal-oral" transmission, meaning some form of the infectious organism is shed in feces and enters a new host or victim by way of the mouth. The *Giardia lamblia* protozoan has a two-stage life cycle. The active stage, the trophozoite, feeds and reproduces in the intestine of the animal host; any live trophozoites excreted in feces die off rapidly. The second stage (the encysted or dormant cyst), also passed in fecal matter, is much hardier and able to survive in an outside environment. When ingested by a new host, each dormant cyst is spring-loaded to *ex*cyst two trophozoites and we start all over.

Direct fecal-oral transmission of *Giardia* cysts is a concern in preschool daycare centers and other institutions. This type of transmission by direct person-to-person contact (and via contaminated food) can easily be eliminated in town and the outback with careful attention to washing hands. It is the waterborne transmission that poses a bigger problem in the wilds. Once the cysts have entered lakes and streams, they can remain viable for months—particularly in cold waters.

Giardia cysts have been discovered in mountain headwaters, the alpine feeders that spring to life from rainfall and snowmelt that eventually wash down to form our watercourses. Concentrations are higher in some rivers and streams than in others; studies show that both occurrence and concentrations change regionally and seasonally. It is still very possible to scoop a cupful of pure water directly from a stream, but the risks aren't worth it. Technically, as soon as water falls from the sky and lands on the ground or bubbles to the surface from a natural spring, it is possible for *Giardia* to be present. Only a few cysts need be ingested and enter our intestinal track to cause infection. In "Eat, Drink, and Be Wary" (reprinted from California Wilderness Coalition in *Headwaters*, Friends of the

River, March/April 1984), Thomas Suk discusses various paths by which fecal material enters wilderness waterways:

> Direct deposition by humans or animals into water, and deposition near water where the cysts can be carried into the water by runoff, rising water levels, erosion, or on the feet of humans and animals. Cysts may also be carried to water on the haircoat of animals who roll in feces.

Giardia is present nowadays in much of the animal kingdom, with strains having been found in fish, birds, reptiles, and many mammalian species. Animal feces continue to contaminate remote watersheds, although it is not completely clear just how many are transferable to humans (or vice versa). Beavers and muskrats, who spend their lives in the water, are known carriers. But the saddest commentary on the disease is that humans more than likely play a substantial role in spreading it to beavers, and to worldwide watersheds.

Prior to 1970, there were no reports in the United States of waterborne outbreaks of *Giardia*. The first came out of Aspen, Colorado, in 1970. Over the next four years, many cases of giardiasis were documented in travelers returning from, of all places, Leningrad. The explanation for this was twofold: the Soviet Union had become more open to visitation by Westerners about that time and Leningrad's municipal water supply was full of *Giardia* cysts. The US outbreak sparked debate and speculation, as well as research, into *Giardia*'s origins and the manner of transmission among species. Where did it come from? Who gave it to whom? Who bears the greatest responsibility for its spread: animals or humans? What do we do now?

A popular theory, seeming to exonerate humans, is that *Giardia* has been around all along—throughout the eons—and is only now being correctly diagnosed. "Around" could be the key word in this theory. *Giardia* might well have been around somewhere, but in the Sierras? In the Rockies? Undeniably, in other parts of the world there have been reports of *Giardia* since it was discovered in 1681. I can't help but recall that numerous river cronies and I drank from watersheds all over the western US and Canada throughout the late 1960s and into the mid-1970s and never came down with *Giardia*—other intestinal disorders on occasion, but not *Giardia*. Only in the late '70s and early '80s did we begin to hear repeatedly of unshakable cases of this "new disease" among us. It seems improbable that we were all previously either asymptomatic carriers or misdiagnosed. Until 1991, New Zealand's wilderness waterways, for reasons not altogether clear, were reportedly *Giardia*-free—possibly because of the country's strict quarantine regulations on all incoming livestock and pets, the island's inherent isolation, and/or the absence of indigenous water mammals. Then, sadly, *Giardia* reached their pristine country's shores. At about the same time, on the opposite end of the earth, another *Giardia*-free pocket succumbed: Nahanni National Park, a remote area (access only by fly-in) in Canada's Northwest Territories.

To further humor my personal suspicions as to where the responsibility for the spread of *Giardia* lies, I offer a few more thoughts. If left solely to the animals in the wild, it seems the progression might have marched along at a different pace, beaver to beaver, stretching over a long period of time—hundreds, even thousands of years (perhaps never to have reached us at all owing to Darwinian selection or a buildup of natural immunities). It is known that both humans and animals can and do spread this disease. There is also evidence to suggest that animals may well rid themselves of *Giardia* during the winter months only to be reinfected by humans in the spring.

Another parasite, with the impressive name *Cryptosporidium* (causing the illness cryptosporidiosis), is also found in backcountry surface waters and sometimes with more frequency and in higher concentrations than *Giardia*. *Cryptosporidium* made headlines in 1993 as the cause of a waterborne outbreak in Milwaukee that affected in the neighborhood of 400,000 people. As a protozoan, it is similar to *Giardia* in all the following ways: fecal-oral transmission, intestinal propagation, viability in water for long periods, passage between humans and animals, characteristics of acute symptoms, potential for chronic affliction, and occurrence of asymptomatic carriers. *Cryptosporidium*, however, is highly resistant to chlorine (much more so than *Giardia*). The estimated twenty-one million Americans who receive municipal drinking water from systems dependent on chlorination, without filtration, are at risk. In other words: don't stay home merely in the hope of avoiding contaminated drinking water.

Before drinking, this is the safest strategy: Treat all backcountry surface water—stream, lake, and waterfall. Treat spring water unless it's contained in a concrete housing that provides security against contamination from surface water and animal feces. Keep in mind that the water is only as good as the housing; springs with old crumbling or cracked housings are suspect. Finally, treat even municipal drinking water in developing countries and also in the United States when advised. Backcountry water treatment systems are discussed in chapter 5.

Now for the roaring voices about whether *Giardia* even *widely* exists? Several times in recent years it's come to my attention that there are quite a number of wilderness trekkers pooh-poohing the notion of widespread *Giardia*. These hikers swear by NOT carrying any field water treatment apparatus. Having to filter water all along the way of an extended hike is, I'll agree, time-consuming and a wholly irksome task when wanting to get back to the simplicities of nature. Surely Jane and Tarzan never interrupted their jungle communing to thump away on a pump. Yet beginning a dialogue with a personal account of not contracting *Giardia*—in, say, a lifetime of tramping the backcountry—and expanding it to mean broader evidence that no one is at risk, is risky in itself. Theories of this kind are often stated with bald adamancy. I also hear less vociferously delivered opinions coming from cherished friends, one of whom has taken to skimming lake water off the surface, with the idea that *Giardia* cysts sink; another drinks water straight from a stream in seasons of low water, but not during spring runoff when he envisions everything washing into waterways; and a third quenches her thirst directly from creeks close to headwaters, but not downstream. The latter two ideas have seeming, but not proven, merit. As for skimming lakes—lake water constantly circulates. If we could remove cysts by allowing water to settle, we'd already be doing it.

Before weighing in any further on this subject, let me state that I hold no stock or options in field water treatment companies and receive no free samples. When in need of equipment, I trot down to my local outdoor store and purchase items outright. Now, commencing with those folks who will even profess to having brought back samples of wilderness water and taken them in for testing: don't believe them! Or, at least, press for further details. For such an undertaking, one not only has to be a bodybuilder but also wealthy. Although stool specimens can be tested quite easily and inexpensively in numerous lab facilities, when it comes to actual wilderness water, a 15-liter sample (more than a half-full 5-gallon bucket) is required for the analysis—imagine someone's lugging that out of the high country, just to prove a point.

But hold on, that's not all. Then you fork over hundreds of dollars. Yes, per test. But say you did this, that you got this far and the test came back negative and you're set to run out and crow around town what you've discovered. What have you really discovered? Simply that *Giardia* cysts were not floating past that certain spot during the moments you were collecting your sample. When the CDC says that *Giardia* is present in all of the world's surface water, they don't mean in every cupful. Remember? It's rather a game of Russian roulette. And there *are* those people, I swear, who have an inordinately powerful Lady Luck riding around in their intestines.

Which leads me to a different batch of stories that have come to my notice—these are from individuals who've been roaming the wilderness for as long as thirty years, drinking freely and never contracting *Giardia*, only finally to find themselves afflicted. I would be inclined to follow, at minimum, the precautions of the dear, late Walkin' Jim Stoltz, longtime long-distance hiker, adventurer, writer, musician, and showman. There was a time, he told me, when he drank straight from any old source—from mud puddles to, accidentally, a stream of toxic waste. Then in the 1980s, in Bryce Canyon National Park, "a nasty bout of gastric ailment," he said, "ruined my walk," although it was not, to his knowledge, caused by *Giardia*. After that, he drank water neat only from carefully scouted sources in the high country and, otherwise, "not wanting to endanger the life of a trip," he carried a small filtration pump.

In my own final analysis of the spread of *Giardia* and *Cryptosporidium*, one earnest issue comes to light above all others: it is a matter of grave import that we—animals, such as we are, and purportedly in possession of notable mental capacity—recognize the potential extent of our impact on the total animal kingdom. Too often, we fail to take fully into account the ramifications of our fast-living, expedient ways, which reverberate through every aspect of life on the planet and boomerang to haunt us.

In retrospect, the appearance of these parasites could be of great benefit to us, if they teach us only that we are capable of spreading odd, new diseases as fast as we take vacations. What animal other than *Homo sapiens* can swallow *rogani gosht* in India or *kalya e khaas* in South Africa and shit it into the Colorado countryside?

Permit me a final muse on the global subject of spreading diseases before we take up our trowels to dig holes. In most of Africa and parts of the Middle East and South America, surface waters are infested with *Schistosoma*, the blood flukes that cause schistosomiasis (also called *Bilharzia* after the discovering physician). The presence of these flukes precludes any swimming or wading, as the manner of entry for the flukes' eggs (or schistosomes) is through the skin. Into these waters, the late, great, environmental activist Edward Abbey would not have dared dip even his parched big toe to cool off. Fortunately for us in North America, one stage of the *Schistosoma*'s life cycle must take place in a snail found only in the tropics. But then again, who out there can promise me that at some future date a minor mutation in the blood fluke's thermostat or, what's more probable, changes in world climate might not leave this parasite completely compatible with our temperate-zone, garden-variety escargot? And if not *Bilharzia*, something else is bound to arrive on our shores.

The best line of defense for protecting our wild lands, our wild friends, and ourselves is to develop scrupulous habits of disposal—plus an environmentally sound hole and bury that shit!—and a compulsion for educating newcomers to the woods with equal fastidiousness.

Let's Go Digging

Oops, **trowels**! A few words here. If you have an older **U-Dig-It**—the palm-size stainless steel trowel with folding handle and belt sheath, a tool sturdy enough to plant trees and dig firelines—hang on to it, guard it with your life! They are now made in China; reports have them snapping closed on fingers and constructed of inferior material, trowel and sheath. Otherwise, perhaps start with SectionHiker.com's gear guide, "5 Best Leave No Trace Trowels of 2019," which selects **The TentLab Deuce of Spades #2** as its top option. Check out all five before deciding. And pull up "The Trowel—Necessary or Nonsense?" on YouTube. Great video! Thanks, Darwinonthetrail.

Choosing a good excavation site for the one-sit hole requires some knowledge and preparation. The overall objective in burying human fecal matter is to inhibit the passing of disease-causing organisms—by humans, interested animals, or storm runoff—into nearby surface waters. And by flying insects back to food areas.

There is no one best set of rules for all terrains, seasons, and climates. In fact, such a collection of variables and trade-offs exists that, at first, it might seem one would need four PhDs to sort them all out. For example, the decomposition rate of buried feces is greatly influenced by all of the following: soil type and texture, filterability (as measured in percolation rates), moisture content, slope of terrain, general exposure, insect inhabitation, soil pH, and temperature.

The trade-offs in environmental protection are between security and decomposition. The ideal spot for rapid decomposition (*rapid* is completely relative here; under the best conditions, human shit can take more than a year to vanish) is in soil that's dry to somewhat moist, but not excessively moist, and has abundant humus and bacteria. To better understand this description, think of the perfect place as being shaded part of the day by vegetation that annually sheds its leaves—but not in a drainage area affected by storm runoff or at a site intermittently inundated by an annual rise in water table.

Feces deposited in extremely parched soils in open locations will not be at much risk of removal by runoff. But this kind of ground is difficult to dig into, and the lack of bacterial activity in the meager topsoil could mean that deposits take nigh on forever to decompose. Above timberline and in subzero climates, bacterial activity is virtually nonexistent. In such spots, it is better to pack out your poop—no kidding!—at least back to where it can be buried in good earth, and most often right on back to the trailhead or home.

The next and most thankful thing to learn about digging is that you're not required to dig to China. Quite the contrary: the most effective enzymes for breaking down excrement live within the top 8 inches of soil. It's generally recommended that you dig down 6 to 8 inches. This allows sufficient coverage of dirt to discourage animal contact and to keep flying insects from vectoring pathogens back to food areas. Products and procedures for group and solo packing-it-out are covered in chapters 3 and 4.

If you're interested in becoming a burying expert or boggling your mind further with all these variables, read Harry Reeves's fascinating article "Human Waste Disposal in the Sierran Wilderness" (*Wilderness Impact Studies*, San Francisco Sierra Club Outing Committee, 1979). For the rest of us, one wise philosopher stated it well, "One can do *only* what one can do," and so it is with the search for the ideal hole. Our goal, therefore, will be to dig holes that are as ecologically sound and as aesthetically pleasing as our layperson's knowledge and the rest of this chapter will allow.

The primary consideration in choosing a burial site is to prevent feces from becoming washed into any waterway. Even when buried, the bacteria in human waste are capable of traveling a good distance through the surrounding soil. Choose a location well away from creeks, streams, and lakes—200 feet is generally recommended, though I find this figure difficult to apply to anything beyond wide-plained rivers and some lakes. (Keep in mind that reservoirs with highly fluctuating water levels are not, as most are named, lakes.) Canyons carved by flowing water have vastly different configurations. With a gently meandering stretch, you could walk away three miles and still remain in the annual flood plain, while in a narrow gorge you might need to climb two stories to find a secure spot.

The best plan is to stay above—well above—the high-water line of spring runoff. This line is not always easy to locate. In some terrain, the high-water line can be as elusive as the other sock—the one you swear went into the dryer. Although with a bit of training, you'll be able to find it.

The great springtime gush of water created by snowmelt usually brings down a load of debris: gravel, rocks, boulders, brush, limbs, even whole trees. Invariably, as flood waters peak, slow, and drop, portions of this debris become beached on open shores or caught in riparian vegetation, settling in a relatively horizontal line. In steep river canyons, as you float along on a late season water level, spring's high-water line can be yards above your head. You might look skyward in mid-river and notice a tree trunk deposited curiously atop a house-size boulder, so high and dry by midsummer you'd guess only giants could have placed it there.

Another clue to the high-water line is a watermark—a bathtub ring—left as a horizontal stain on a canyon's rock walls. And then some watercourses rage only in spring or during flash floods from thunderstorms and are bone-dry the remainder of the year. Learn to develop an eye for terrain and drainages—the low spots, the canyon bottoms, the erosion gullies, the dry washes. Ask knowledgeable locals to acquaint you with how high a river will rise during the spring runoff. Gradually, you'll learn to estimate the level fairly accurately from the shape and steepness of a canyon. When in doubt, climb higher; next year might be the cyclical big one—the twenty-five-year flood, the hundred-year flood.

Winter landscapes require more skill on our part. Spring's high-water line is obliterated under drifts of snow. Terrain is difficult to determine, and the chances of squatting on top of a buried streambed increase when you are not familiar with an area from previous summer visits. Steer clear of flat, open places, because they might be frozen ponds or wide meadows, the latter being a mountain's flood plains that gather and funnel water into creeks. The best advice is to head for the high ground. In deep snowpack or subzero temperatures, when you can't dig into the frozen earth or sometimes even dig far enough to find earth, the recommendation again is to pack-it-out.

The Merits and Methods of Stirring

Stirring, or "the mix-master method" as it is sometimes called, is a brilliant technique that we all need to learn and employ. It is that "mixing" of the item we've deposited in our one-sit hole with loose dirt scraped from the sides of the hole before covering it over, all to the purpose of enhancing the decomposition rate by way of bringing soil bacteria into contact with a greater portion of the turd. Use a small stick for this purpose, something you can drop into the hole, not a tool you will be returning to your belt sheath or backpack. Think ahead. Pick up a downed stick along the way to your mission site, and when first digging the hole, loosen some dirt from the sides. Where sticks are in short supply, be creative. Use a stone. Carry a few Popsicle sticks you don't mind parting with. Be aware that "no sticks" might mean a high-use area that's been combed clean, an area with no bacteria in the soil, or an area with no soil—situations, once again, where packing-it-out is environmentally preferable to burying it.

The merits of stirring come to us as far back as 1982 in a study conducted in Montana's Bridger Range (Kenneth L. Temple, Anne K. Camper, and Robert C. Lucas, "Potential Health Hazard from Human Wastes in Wilderness," *Journal of Soil and Water Conservation*, Vol. 37, No. 6, November/December 1982). Fecal matter inoculated with bacterial pathogens *E. coli* and *Salmonella* was buried in cat holes. *Salmonella* proved a hardy survivor at all sites over the winter; *E. coli* persisted at some. The researchers theorized that fecal matter might actually insulate bacteria from the breakdown action of soil and proposed that mixing soil and feces might speed up die-off. But no one then could imagine backcountry recreationists employing such a practice. Now here we are . . . closing in on three decades of stirring!

Latrines: If You Must

Digging a group latrine is indicated only on very rare occasions. I cringe at the thought of sharing how to build latrines, and for that reason did not include it in the first edition of this book. Then more than several people inquired. With the idea here that it's better to have the best information and not use it than to ignorantly spade up random plots, I lay it out again—though not without considerable trepidation. Large, concentrated deposits of fecal matter break down extremely slowly. You mustn't head into the woods with the casual thought, Oh, we'll just dig a big old pit. Excavating a latrine will disturb a large area of plant life. In most places nowadays, a latrine will be environmentally inappropriate; you will need to come prepared to pack out all the human waste your group generates (again see chapter 3).

It's the highly unusual circumstance that requires a latrine. One situation comes to mind: I was recently reminded there's an age, somewhere between infancy and adulthood, characterized by squeamishness and fits of giggling embarrassment. Generally, groups of this maturity level remain close to base camp facilities. But if you find yourself in the boondocks as the leader of such a group, and you're not sufficiently assured that cat holes will be dug in a proper manner, then a closely monitored latrine might be in order. When you're giving out instructions, keep in mind that embarrassment and squeamishness are cultural phenomena and will not disappear until adults become more direct in their own approach to the subject.

Think of a latrine as a multiperson cat hole, as opposed to a coffin-size landfill. It needs to be easily accessible, closer to camp than a remote cat hole might be, and with some type of screening for privacy. The rest of the location considerations are similar to cat holes. Stay far away from boggy areas, springs, meadows, wetlands—200 feet from lakes and well above a river's high-water line. Keep out of dry washes that might carry storm runoff. In other words, again go for the high ground. Study the terrain and visualize where water might flow. Even in a desert, water leaves signs: slick rocks are a giveaway, because water has probably polished them.

Situate the latrine in soil with exceptionally good humus. The disadvantages of large deposits are a higher concentration of pathogens in one place and a slower rate of breakdown. Excavate a shallow (6- to 8-inch), narrow (8- to 10-inch) trench that people can straddle and squat over. To determine the length of your latrine, take into account the size of your group and the length of stay. Underestimate—you can always dig up a couple more feet. Pile the dirt alongside the length of the trench. Instruct people to begin at one end; after each deposit, shovel in a dusting of soil, stir energetically, then cover well and tamp down. A communal stick for stirring can be conveniently left sticking into the used section of the trench, stirring end down. Ever hear the expression "shit end of the stick"? This is the stick they were talking about. (In the old days, it had a rag attached to one end for cleaning chamber pots.) Finally, station a paper bag for refuse handy to squatters. Later it will be packed out. From cat hole to latrine, the real mastery lies in the artistry of returning the landscape to the look it had before you started—more easily done when your hole is small.

In the end, we all have a decision to make about our methods of sanitation. The procedure we choose will depend upon the size of the season and climate, the remoteness of the location, the visitation intensity, and on and on. The easier we make it on ourselves, the harder it will be on Mother Earth. A fair portion of determination may be required at some bends in the trail, but take heart: we're all learning together—about something we all do.

Game Plan for T.P.

Let's focus for a moment on the subject of toilet paper. A rock climber once related the story of finding herself clinging to a ledge halfway up Yosemite's Half Dome when that urge we know so well suddenly came upon her. Rock climbing was then the least regulated of outback activities, and rock climbers were notorious for just letting it fly, bombs away! It wasn't uncommon to hear stories of climbers who'd been hit on the head. But in this instance, the climb was (as more and more are) organized to be respectful of the mountain and other climbers. Remaining safely in her leg loops, she somehow skillfully peeled down her pants and positioned her carryout container. Next, she ripped off an arm's length of toilet tissue, promptly lost her grasp of it, and watched it quietly float away. The escaped streamer curled downward for only a moment before being snatched by an updraft. For the better part of an hour—soaring, diving, looping, happy as a mime artist—this tail of tissue entertained everyone strung across Half Dome. Need I say more about hanging on to your t.p.?

Actually yes, two more cautions. **Don't bury it. Don't burn it.** Burning was the accepted practice for some years, but the thinking has now changed. No matter how careful you think you might be, one accidental forest fire is one too many. Use as little paper, therefore, as you can manage, and then pack it all out. To better encourage this practice when camped with others, it's helpful to provide instructions and a discreet location for collection. A paper bag can be stationed at the outer edge of camp along with a roll of t.p. and a shovel.

It should go without saying to pack out all other inorganic accoutrements of toiletry: tampons, sanitary pads, and diapers. If you are washing diapers on a trip, dispose of the actual ca-ca in one-sit holes dug in the manner previously described. Haul the wash bucket above the high-water line and use only biodegradable soap. In rinsing out the wash bucket, use another pan or bucket to avoid rinsing directly in the stream. Pour the wash water into a hole (again, above the high-water line) and cover with dirt. Even with biodegradable soap, don't wash directly in a watercourse.

What about Pee?

A trekker's urine is an altogether different affair. Pee evaporates rapidly and is relatively sterile, unless a bladder infection is present (and a sufferer would be well aware of such a condition). The major cautions with peeing are to keep away from high-use areas where the stench becomes unpleasant and to avoid peeing on gravel where urine will leave a lasting odor. In certain areas, notably Grand Canyon beaches, the National Park Service instructs people to pee directly into the river or on the wet sand at water's edge. The pee is then washed away by daily fluctuations in water level connected with Glen Canyon Dam, upstream. The pee-in-the-river procedure was not adopted solely to eliminate rank urine smells; the concentration of pee (containing nitrogen) that boaters would otherwise deposit in soils of the Grand Canyon—an arid and slow-changing environment—would rapidly alter the soil chemistry and, in turn, the native vegetation. The volume of river water in the Colorado, upward of 15,000 cubic feet per second, also warrants this practice. Over the course of a year, that amounts to about one part pee to about fifty-five million parts water—or, as once calculated by Mark Law, a National Park Service district manager, the equivalent of twenty-eight thousand cases of beer. Follow this procedure, however, only when the park or forest service specifically requests it.

For *any* type of eliminating, wander a good distance (minimum 200 feet) from a camp area, not only for privacy but also to avoid squatting on potential sleeping spots or kitchen sites. If you're moving your camp every day, use this to advantage by making deposits in the areas of least visitation along your route. This is called "elimination on the move." Stay away from the edges of trails, which are in themselves high-use areas. Plan ahead, or you'll find yourself skipping off the path at the first available nook—one that doubtless had the same appeal to many before you. Certain regions are predictably deep in shit, such as the scouting trails just upstream of hellbender rapids. (Nothing gets bowels moving faster than worrying you might die.)

Ocean Disposal

Ocean saltwater has long been considered a different story than fresh water. It's customary when sea kayaking to void in a can, toss the contents overboard, rinse out the can, and resume paddling. Or there's the option of jumping overboard, provided you are practiced in solo rescue and can haul yourself back in. On ecological grounds, some sea-touring groups have recommended water disposal, even for *number two*, over waiting for a beach disposal. There are boaters who'll argue that disposal of shit in water around island communities is safe when it's tossed into a moving, deep-water channel of 12 feet or more. Yet the casual vacation kayaker (me) paddling in a maze of channels will find it difficult to ascertain depth beneath a bobbing boat. What's more, a knowledge of tides is involved or, instead of flushing out to sea, your "turd overboard" could wash right back onto favored clam beds.

The idea of *aqua dumps* or *shit-puts*, as they're called, runs contrary to all fibers of my being. Recollection of a water experience in Mexico reinforces my resistance. Someone once handed me a cheap ticket to Acapulco and I arrived on the lovely tropical beaches only to be warned not to swim in the bay's polluted waters. Too much raw sewage, it seemed. When the heat became oppressive, I swam in the hotel's pool—might as well have been side-stroking through chlorination at home.

By federal law, oceangoing vessels are prohibited from dumping sewage inside the three-mile zone from shore. A kayak is but a one-person/one-coffee-can yacht. With sea kayakers paddling our coasts in increasing numbers, typically touring close to islands and through small bays, or weaving through estuaries where wildlife viewing is best, it is this author's recommendation, on a planet already overburdened with excrement—where we're also facing such monstrous things as oil spills, balloons turning up in dead marine animals' intestines, ocean garbage patches growing twice the size of Texas, rising sea levels, soaring prices of scallops, sea creature extinctions—that fecal matter never be tossed overboard. But at least not inside the three-mile zone of the mainland or the most seaward island in a group of islands. Packing-it-out, transporting it home for sewage treatment, is the preferred course of action. Second best—a cat hole dug in vegetation above the beach—is reasonable on occasion (see page 36, for fragility of small islands). There is no law that says sea kayakers can't set the example for the rest of the world. The ocean herself is saying, "Enough!"

So make sure to pack your trowel and a feasible container (see chapter 4) before setting out to sea like the Owl and the Pussycat in your beautiful pea-green boat.

3

When You Can't Dig a Hole

In days of old
When knights were bold
And toilets weren't invented
They left their load
Along the road
And walked off so contented.

—A childhood ditty; author unknown

In the pursuit of unknowns, a ranging world explorer can throw open entire new universes, not to mention some curious dimensions of toiletry and disposal. Sometimes there's just no place to dig a hole. Most of us never have occasion to pray that we won't have to go big potty outside when it's forty below or while dangling in midair between pitons on a thousand-foot rock face. In all probability, we are home knitting, walking the dog, or watching the Super Bowl. Of course, anyone trudging on foot to the South Pole or climbing Mount Everest is already committed to a multitude of unpleasantries. These breeds of outdoor enthusiasts are extraordinary souls; pride in their accomplishments does not spring from enduring the familiar. The morning constitutional performed behind the morning paper may be an ordinary, even enjoyable, task when at home. But under adverse conditions, this simple activity can turn into a colossal calamity or feat of contortion. Consider the mishap that Sir Chris Bonington endured at 26,000 feet during an ascent on Everest, as described in his book *The Ultimate Challenge* (New York: Stein & Day, 1963):

> Now we've got these one-piece down suits; it's not too bad, in fact it's comparatively easy to relieve oneself when wearing the down suit by itself. If, however, you are wearing the down suit and the outer suit, it is absolutely desperate, trying to get the two suits to line up. . . . Afterwards, without thinking, without looking back, I stood up and shoved my windproof suit back on. . . . I did not realize anything was wrong until I poked my hand through the cuff! I tried to scrape it off—rub it off—but by this time the sun had gone, it was bitterly cold and it had frozen to the consistency of concrete.

Sir Chris is to be hailed for sharing this private predicament; it provides solace, after the fact, for anyone in the misery-loves-company category, and it serves to forewarn the rest of us of one disastrous route to humiliation.

Next take note of this dismayed woman, who also bought a suit of misery. A robust friend of mine was camped in Oregon's Three Sisters during a blizzard, when an imperious peristaltic contraction indicated it was time to crawl out of the tent and squat. So—out she ventured into a complete whiteout, snow blowing horizontally on a wicked wind. Five layers of clothes had to be stripped from her rosy behind and shoved below her knees. Never mind the freezing; in retrieving her pants she found that each layer, not unlike a birdbath, had captured a supply of snow. Once the clothes were again clasped to her body, the snow began to melt. Winter campers call it the "soggies." When questioned as to whether she might not have some helpful hint for others caught in such circumstances, her only reply was "Hold it!"

Two timeworn solutions to the undeniable problems associated with winter camping do offer themselves. Trapdoors decidedly provide some buttress against inclement weather. Fashioned after the old union suits with their fanny drop-flaps, various styles are available in heavy expedition wear. And the other merciful aid in subzero temperatures? Just what *did* great-grandma do when the weather was too bitter to pad along in her bare feet and flannel nightie to the outhouse? Ah, the old porcelain chamber pot—the "thunder mug," as it was called. Less elegantly, coffee cans have been used. And a variety of imaginative newer solutions will appear as we move through the next chapters.

Of course, not all extreme adventures issue forth from remote high and cold country. Another friend, an expedition leader, was once caught in rush-hour gridlock on the fourth level of a freeway interchange. It was, thankfully, only a *number one* emergency; he filled his thermos four times and casually dumped the contents out the window. From a reliable female source, I've heard that snap-shut plastic bread savers have been put to the same front-seat use on long cross-country hauls across barren landscapes. Nowadays, you can purchase all sorts of fancy unisex, disposable, or multiple-use urine-gelling containers. Just search for pee bags online. Chapter 6 offers in-depth guidance and accessories for women's stand-up peeing, turning our backs to the traffic—just like men. As for me? I'd rather pull to the shoulder, park my old pickup with its tailgate angled slightly toward the shoulder (to provide cover from behind), then swing open the passenger door (blocking the view from oncoming traffic) and sit on what today suffices for a running board. Human ingenuity is a savior when you can't hold it for another minute.

But along with ingeniousness, we have our weaknesses, our blind spots, and then our fastidious aversions to anything leaning toward fecal ickiness, which can translate into a mighty mess for Mother Earth. With numbers of both hardy explorers and casual backcountry travelers continuing to swell around the globe, we are forced to grapple with the identical sanitation problems of T. J. Crapper's nineteenth century. Too much stuff, no good place for it to go. No matter how conscientious people become about carting their trash and food garbage back to trailheads, each wave of visitors still leaves, in addition to footprints, shit. You can only cram so many apples into a barrel and then the barrel is full. And our dear Mother is screaming.

The ever-growing feeling in the outdoor community is that we can no longer afford—like knights of old—to leave our load along the road. Rudely cared-for feces can be a fierce affront to our aesthetics and a threat to our health. For example: Grievously noticeable to early spring backpackers are the turdly remains of the previous season's visitors. With snow's melting, the frozen lumpettes left by cross-country skiers sit plunk on top of the ground. The weather warms and they thaw and ripen along with the rest of the landscape. For an early hiker who is seeking a few days of solace in untrammeled places, this is a horrific sight. One might better have stayed home and scheduled a tour of the local sewage treatment plant.

Sometimes, leaving behind even the most properly buried deposits can cause irreparable ecological damage. Small islands, for instance, have tenuous ecosystems at best. The fragility of islands is inherent: they have no adjacent support system. Off the coast of Maine lie three thousand islands, many no bigger than an isolated acre. The interdependence of life on an acre island—what looks to us to be grasses and a couple of trees—has been in the making for millions of years. Now visitors come, and not just in the form of the odd fisherman or lovers picnicking, but sea kayakers by the dozen camping overnight, or tour groups off chartered schooners, sometimes thirty at a time, stopping for a landside lunch. Too many cat holes, too much disturbed earth, and the grasses vanish, leaving topsoil to the mercy of wind and weather. It's far better for us to tread gently than be confronted later with another in the long line of mitigations—not always successful mitigations—we now face.

The ecosystems of caves are another example of isolated and delicately balanced flora and fauna. Caves often shelter vulnerable and delightfully bizarre little creatures found nowhere else on earth. For the spelunker, in addition to the seriousness of species interdependence, there is the compelling subject of rank odors. The true cave-lover looks upon the removal of bodily waste as merely one step in heedful exploration.

A sensitive ecosystem that's not always so evident, even to those best informed, is the wetland. Washington state's King County touts a 100-page Sensitive Areas Ordinance that creates buffer zones of 25 to 100 feet around three different classifications of wetlands, ruling out, among other things, septic systems. The ordinance contains no specifications for an individual camper's deposits; nonetheless, local environmentally minded sea kayakers using cat-hole methods find occasion to crow, "Know your wetland plants!" Not so easy, I was once told by Ken Carrasco, a King County environmental educator. "Of all the environmentally sensitive areas, the most difficult to delineate and classify are wetlands." Their vegetation can stretch beyond obvious swampy specimens like eelgrass and cattails to trees of western red cedar, black cottonwood, and Sitka spruce that inhabit "forested wetlands." Only seven days of inundation during the growing season (in the Seattle area, March to November) are necessary to set the stage for the survival of a wetland species. And wetlands vary greatly in size, some taking up no more space than an office file cabinet. The title of a chapter from *Wetland Plants of the Pacific Northwest*, an Army Corps of Engineers' publication, says it all: "Wetland Identification Complexities: Life Is Not Simple."

The Evolution of Packing-It-Out

"Packing-it-out"—the practice of capturing and transporting fecal matter, and sometimes pee, out of the backcountry—is currently the sensible alternative to burial in areas of high-use and fragile ecosystems. As early as 1988, Cal Adventures (CA), the outdoor program at the University of California at Berkeley, under the direction of Rick Spittler, began experimenting with individual containerization systems for participants in their cross-country skiing program. CA's novel techniques were successful, if rudimentary: milk cartons with duct tape. These days, day hikers on busy high-country trails are sometimes given space-age "bags" for turd disposal and carry-out. Conscientious sea kayakers, in many parts of the world, are paddling their solid eliminations home. The US Forest Service straps portable toilets onto mules that accompany trail crews into the mountains. The big outdoor schools, Colorado Outward Bound and the National Outdoor Leadership School, teach packing-it-out. Mountaineers, on favorite heavily traveled routes, have jumped on the clean wilderness effort. Even rock climbers (fed up with oversized hail?) are changing their ways. Antarctic expeditions now pack-it-out. Every year, participation in this cleanup campaign is made easier by a growing overall consciousness—everybody in the same poo boat—and the development of specialized equipment, not to mention tightening regulations. For the rest of this chapter, we will temporarily decamp from the needs of individual poop-packers and turn our focus to *groups* and their portable shitarees.

Some fifty years ago, it was whitewater boaters who emerged as the first *parties* of wilderness-goers to experiment with hauling human feces out of pristine areas. River terrain poses unique problems, with overnight camping often confined by the naturally limited beaches of steep and narrow canyons, or by privately owned adjacent land. When the sport of "shooting the rapids" grew in popularity, the increase in human visitation was subsequently followed by tremendous concentrations of fecal matter. The need to pack-it-out became evident when people began digging up others' "stuff" in an effort to bury their own.

Since 1979, all solid human excreta from Grand Canyon river trips has been containerized and removed. The River Permit Office for the Grand Canyon issues trip leaders two full pages of instructions about packing-it-out. On Canyon beaches, there's the potential for 200,000 deposits per year, or roughly 50 tons of shit. Picture, purely for the sake of comprehension, finding 200,000 helpings of spaghetti and meatballs buried in the sand. With that image, the National Park Service's regulations become perfectly understandable. No trip is allowed on the river without ample approved holding tanks, proper education, and a commitment to leaving behind no human poop.

It wasn't long before these regulations spread to other heavily run rivers. When removal was adopted in 1983 on Idaho's Main Salmon (Lewis and Clark's famed River of No Return),

Bob Abbott, then district ranger of Nez Perce National Forest, was nothing short of skeptical about public cooperation. As a second-generation ranger, born even in a ranger district, Abbott had spent years observing the behavior of *Homo sapiens* in the wild. Tin Can Tourists, as litterbugs were called in the days before plastic, couldn't be counted on to pack out even the smallest bits of trash. Abbott's reaction to the idea of expecting visitors to haul out their excrement was "You gotta be kidding! We'll have shit from hell to breakfast!" But he rapidly became a convert and then instrumental in promotion, getting a SCAT Machine (see page 40) installed in Riggins, Idaho, near the Main Salmon's take-out. By 2011, he was emanating downright pride in telling me, "You can visit a beach that's had seven thousand visitors in the space of two months and see no sign that humans have been there." Upon retirement, Abbott traveled to Washington, DC, where he was presented with the award for Excellence in Wild River Management by then Vice President Al Gore.

But suddenly, in October 1993, procedures changed. Packing-it-out got kicked upstairs, when, in what turned out to be a momentous decision, the Environmental Protection Agency (EPA) outlawed the dumping of human fecal matter into landfills. Although not a law enacted with wilderness-goers in mind, it greatly and immediately affected us. As an EPA representative back then explained, "Sewage must go where it can be treated—into sewage treatment plants, sewers, or septic tanks."

Up to that point, the classic toilet system for river runners had been an inexpensive (then, $15) World War II ammunition can, commonly called an *ammo can* or *rocket box*, and easily acquired at most any surplus store. Their lids clamp down vicelike onto a rubber gasket, creating a secure seal against spillage. When in use, a can was lined with a plastic garbage bag, and a toilet seat positioned on top. Presto, outdoor potty! The toilet seat was often omitted on gear-light private trips, which led to the toilet's lasting moniker *groover*, from the parallel furrows left in a sitter's bum.

With recycled rocket boxes, boaters hauled literally thousands of pounds of human waste out of river canyons. But always, awaiting them at take-outs was a big glitch—no facility equipped to receive bagged shit. Plastic bags, which don't biodegrade rapidly, are incompatible with septic tanks and sewage treatment plants. They particularly gum up the works in the honey wagons that pump out trailhead vault toilets.

After caring for their cargoes of turds—painstakingly removing them from camps, ferrying them down rivers, bearing them across beaches, and packing them into vehicles—stymied rafters ended up hurling a goodly percentage of those bulging bags into open pits on someone's south forty. At best, the bags were trucked for miles to a sewage treatment plant, where the contents were poured out and the soiled bags dropped in the trash. At worst, and not uncommon, came the woeful tales of river guides who feared they were doomed to driving a vehicle permanently laden with the infamous freight. Many a moonless landscape, a handy Dumpster, or a lonesome spot in the road caught their share of fling-it-and-run's. Something was terribly awry when the most environmentally conscious bunch around—whitewater boaters—were stuck with no better solution.

The EPA, as many saw it, had come to the rescue. Its ruling, however inadvertently, confronted the big void (pun intended) in sewage facilities at take-outs and trailheads. It served to force progress beyond plastic garbage bags, because even if you were to pour the fecal matter down the pipe at an RV station, you still had to contend with the soiled bag. Not everyone had the iron stomach required to launder one. Thus, what followed was an all-around brainstorming that continues to this day.

The Wizardly SCAT Machine

The **SCAT Machine**, invented by wizard river guide John Witzel, is an overall marvel in disposal. A shiny pearl of history resides inside this shitty bizness: in the beginning, SCAT stood for Sanitizing Containers Alternative Technology, but the acronym has since evolved—not devolved—into Shit Crap And That! Essentially an industrial-size dishwasher hooked into a sewer system, it neatly dumps and cleans most any portable, reusable backcountry toilet—the 5-gallon buckets, box-type potties, even your septic tank if you can dig it out of the ground, but indeed anything with at least an 8-inch top opening and a recommended minimum height of 13 inches. (Containers 1 1¾ to 12 inches tall work marginally, but anything shorter doesn't empty properly.) Just bring your full container and your own strapping to secure it. Remove the container's lid and place it on the accessory wash rack. Closing the machine causes it to swing through a one-eighty turn and ship the holding tank's contents down the sewer. If the price is not already covered in your permit, drop in a few quarters or tokens and the apparatus washes and sanitizes your tank and all but reaches out and hands it back to you.

Installation sites for a standard SCAT Machine require an existing sewer or a septic and leach line system, a 220V power source, and a water supply. Depending on added bells and whistles, prices range from $67,500 to $90,000. The higher-end prices cover items such as attached grinders and solar panels. Witzel will deck out washers with an alarm, one even phones its owner when the machine needs attention. He laughs, "I haven't equipped any with drink holders and stereos yet."

SCAT Machines generally sell to federal agencies (Bureau of Land Management, US Forest Service, and National Park Service) or to a group of commercial outfitters. They serve mostly river runners in their locations in Meadview, AZ; Asotin, WA; Riggins and North Fork, ID; Maupin, Heritage Landing, and Foster Bar, OR, and Happy Camp, CA. The one at the marina in Priest Lake, Idaho, is for campers returning from the islands.

Witzel, being partial to the bomb-proof 20 mm ammo cans (and it's not like we're ever going to run out of them), is designing new SCAT Machines to accept them without strapping—that is, once you've added two minor tab-plate modifications. The Idaho stations are already equipped for this. Folks interested in modifying their 20 mm ammo cans are invited to call the wizard.

SCAT Machine
www.scatmachine.com
39269 Highway 205
Frenchglen, OR 97736
✉ info@scatmachine.com
☎ 541-589-0777

Birth of the Soil Can

The Baker City BLM office in Oregon will go down in history for their stellar, inventive leadership in packing-it-out. Kevin McCoy, former outdoor recreation manager, and Kevin Hoskins, then lead river ranger on designated Wild & Scenic stretches of the Grande Ronde, the Wallowa, and the Powder, worked together on back-country human waste management for more than twenty years. Watching regulations stiffen, they nudged along experimental pack-it-out systems, once nearly buying everything on the market to acquaint their rangers with different products. Meanwhile, visitation on public lands was tripling and federal agencies were unable to keep pace with the expense of maintaining enough toilet facilities. When the Grande Ronde corridor shifted to "mandatory" packing-it-out in 2000, McCoy saw it as an opportunity to place stewardship, more appropriately, in the lap of users—rivers runners, ATVers, and horse packers.

At first, they faced highly unwilling participants. A party of river runners, coming off a five-day trip, showed up at the take-out with an empty potty and bald-faced claims that "no one had to go." But eventually, the Kevins birthed a huge success story. Over the years, their rangers left behind the lousy chore of trail and campsite cleanup—that is, shoveling up clumps of shit and toilet paper—and moved to happily engaging the public in commonplace conversations about how to care for human excreta . . . and getting compliance! "The no-way-you're-going-to-make-me-crap-in-a-bucket folks are now carrying around facilities in their vehicles," McCoy had cheered. All it took was an ordinary 5-gallon hardware-store bucket with a couple of minor accessories and a small bag of potting soil. Plus, of course, a group of dedicated, well-versed rangers comfortable with toilet talk. This is a system that's monumentally user-friendly and inexpensive. For key instructions, see the Do-It-Yourself Soil Can by the Baker City BLM (page 52).

But the Kevins' system is only an example of what has transpired. As might be guessed—with new frontiers, creativity, and adventurers' eternal callings—rising to the occasion of the EPA ruling came a spate of inventors, all scurrying to produce a washable, reusable container that was also user-friendly, as in requiring the least holding of the nose. For a while, a new design appeared almost every week. Now there's been a settling out, with some models disappearing and others taking hold.

As we begin comparing the merits of different systems, toward the idea of purchasing one, there *is* one alternative—in case you're wondering—to all this lugging around of poop. Though not something I personally recommend, I present it here and leave it for you to decide. The suggestion arrived in one of the many letters I receive, a correspondent I've since duly dubbed the Enema Man. In a short typed note, he graciously shared his practice of holing up in a motel to flush his colon the night before striking out on a weekend of fishing. This enables him to roam about untroubled by the particulars of how to squat in the woods, leaving him to concentrate solely on his sport, while—he writes in all sincerity—simultaneously "avoid[ing] polluting the streams and their environs." If this appeals to you, read no further. Hand this book to a neighbor! The rest of us, not so charmed, will move on to other solutions and examining holding tanks.

Choosing a Portable Toilet—Points to Ponder

Beginning on page 48 are the manufacturers of washable-reusable backcountry toilets, because most manufacturers are small operations and it seems certain that encouraging the use of their products is uppermost in the cosmic plan. Although I've added a few comments about each model, this is not meant to be an exhaustive evaluation; design revisions occur frequently and, to be fair, I have not climbed onto all of them. The very act of plopping down on one reveals a critical characteristic: how readily the toilet tips over. And this, believe me, is important. Once a contraption containing the crap of fourteen people throws you to the ground and tries to bury you, there's a good chance you'll turn into a couch potato for life.

When purchasing a portable toilet, there are numerous things to watch for and weigh. Pick and choose the design features that most suit you. You can't have everything with the cheaper models, but sometimes you don't need everything. Off the top, there are a number of important aspects to consider: price; your health; container stability, sturdiness, and quality of seal; dumping and cleaning; "disgust factor"; and length of trip and size of group.

Price: Starting with the simplest aspect to suss out, current prices range from around $25 and $40-ish to $767. After a general discussion here, products are presented from high end to low, along with the Do-It-Yourself Soil Can and the few companies who offer rentals.

Health: Handling toilets is not a business to be taken lightly, and any potential for direct exposure to fecal matter during the setting up, packing up, emptying, or cleaning processes should be carefully considered. When drawing the short straw for potty duty, wearing latex gloves is a wise precaution, but also one lamentably ironic. Proud as we are about diminishing our consumption of plastic bags, we seem to be tying our next Gordian knot around a mountain of latex gloves. The alternative is a good soap-and-water scrub. Health is definitely the priority for the clean-out staff.

Some holding tanks, upon opening, will "burp in your face." Methane gas is a natural by-product of anaerobic decomposing feces. Be forewarned: a sealed holding tank—full or partially full—left in the sun can blow up. Fireworks of that caliber have the potential to psychologically brand a person for life. Short of actual explosion, tanks can also bubble and cough and emit world-class farts. Having an automatic pressure-release mechanism is a decided advantage on long or hot-weather trips. If yours is a courageous spirit, however, tanks without pressure-release valves are generally cheaper and you can crack the lid occasionally, remembering to pack your gear so the lid is accessible. Be advised that peeing in the potty contributes to methane buildup, but not peeing in it can make the dumping difficult at trip's end.

There are two schools of thought on content consistency: the wet and the dry. The dry group is acutely aware that liquids add to weight and prefers to collect only solid waste, adding water at the completion of a trip. The wet group believes in brewing a sort of slurry that will easily pour. Sometimes, only women on the trip are instructed to pee in the pot; other times, all guests are told to pee elsewhere, while the guides discreetly monitor and maintain a good consistency.

Shape, stability, sturdiness, and seals: Next to ponder is container shape: round, square, or oblong. Consider how your gear is packed. A round object, if not entirely sturdy, can eventually assume a square shape when squished by dunnage. And consider stability. A bucket, because its top is larger in diameter than its bottom, will be less stable to sit on than a container of squatter and squarer design.

Other high priorities are sturdiness in construction material and top-of-the-line seals at all the openings. If a boat flips in a "mother" rapid, there should be no chance of a holding tank leaking during "may-tagging" in a souse hole. Seals must pass what I'm now calling the Donnie Dove Test, giving DDT a whole new meaning. Dove is Canyon REO's (River Equipment Outfitters) expert on leakage. A man with a purpose, he packs a gallon of water seemingly wherever he goes, pouring it into the latest inventions and turning them upside down. Dove espouses a simple but profound axiom: if it can't hold water, it shouldn't hold shit! At last count, not all passed his test.

Dumping and cleaning: Eventually, you must think about the end of your trip and the task of dumping the holding tank. Compatibility with the SCAT Machine is a plus when you are planning to be near one of the few on the planet; otherwise, compatibility with RV dumping stations is a *must*. The latter is achieved by attaching a garden hose at one opening, a sewer hose at another, and blasting fresh water through the tank. Some tanks are not equipped with orifices that fit a freshwater hose. The flushing is instead accomplished through the larger toilet-seat hole, which can produce unsanitary splash back. You can remedy that, somewhat, by fashioning a large rubber washer through which you insert the hose.

Sewage cleaning services come highly recommended as a way of entirely avoiding the clean-out chore. With this news, I called around the rural area where I live and found no such service. I was, in fact, alarmed to discover that the portable plastic out-houses, the ones seen lined up at all manner of public events, were cleaned merely with squirts of cold water. Towns near take-outs for popular river runs are probably better bets. In any case, it's worth the call—if nothing else, it might inspire someone to propose an updating of public health standards. Another choice for disposal is a sewage treatment plant. There the contents of a holding tank are poured through an open grate, but mucking out the container is left to you.

Be aware that plastics more readily absorb odors than do stain-less steel and aluminum, but any container when used regularly will take on a whiff. To help, toss a half-cup of baking soda into cleaned tanks that are sitting around between trips.

"Disgust factor": If your group is large or your trip long, you will need more than one holding tank. When calculating vol-ume, be sure to allow for not only actual space but also what is termed "disgust factor." Using the same container for more than two or three days, or until topped off, will gag almost anyone: instinctual approach/avoidance conflict mode prompts most of us to peer down the hole before sitting. In addition, there are the critical matters of tidal waves and splash back, and for gentlemen, the safety of those forever dangling darlings. Prized is the toilet-seat mounting that provides for perching well above the can's contents. Deodorizers, or "sweeteners" as they're called, also help minimize disgust factor.

Length of trip and container capacity: Another term to know is *user-day*, which means one person, one day. In other words, fifty user-days could mean five people shitting for ten days or ten people shitting for five days, or even fifty people shitting for one day. Capacities noted are not calculated by any standardized method, but given in accordance with the manufacturer's advertising. Some are for poops per can, some for people per day no matter what they are eating, and some for full-to-the-brim tanks.

Try as I might, I found it difficult to establish the size of an "average" poop. It's not the open-and-shut case implied by Woody Guthrie's infamous line in the movie *Bound for Glory*: "The more you eat, the more you shit." In medical encyclopedias, there is a hesitancy to commit to a one-figure average, the worldwide range of normalcy being broad. Anyone who takes a dump three to twenty-one times per week can be considered normal. An individual's product is dependent on age, size of physical frame, diet, gender, genetics, geography, and even personality. People who eat more fiber produce more bulk. Men, as a rule, produce more than women. A typical stool in India weighs three times that of one in England or the United States, whereas in Uganda turd poundage is *five* times greater.

Those of us devoted to the eternal process of "getting our shit together" might be surprised to learn that although our shit might be stinking less, it probably weighs more; the fifth edition of *Gastrointestinal Disease: Pathophysiology, Diagnosis, Management* by Sleisenger and Fordtran (Philadelphia: W. B. Saunders, 1993), tells us that people with high self-esteem produce heavier stools. There's a proverb or fortune cookie riddle in here somewhere, I know it. Something like: Too much psychotherapy makes for weighty business! Thankfully, Carol Hupping Stoner takes a stab at averages for us in *Goodbye to the Flush Toilet: Water-Saving Alternatives to Cesspools, Septic Tanks, and Sewers* (Emmaus, PA: Rodale Press, 1977), calculating daily human excrement at one-half pound, moist weight. That should help—the half-pounder having become a worldwide institution.

A little more advice? Carry a DDT gallon of water and ask a lot of questions.

Washable, Reusable Carry-Out Toilet Systems

The prices quoted here are retail and don't include shipping. Any dimensions given are for holding tanks alone—sometimes inside measurements, sometimes outside—without a seat assembly.

Ammo cans and rocket boxes are designated in millimeters, which refers to the type of ammunition originally stored in them, not the size of the can: for instance, a 30 mm is smaller than a 25 mm.

Jon-ny Partner ($767) is what many call the Cadillac of portable toilets, a bombproof, aluminum holding tank. The price includes the tank with an automatic pressure-release valve; a transport lid with rubber gasket and collar clamp; a toilet seat with a lid; and a flush kit for RV dumping stations (consisting of a clamp-on funnel with a ¾-inch opening for a garden hose, an inside sprayer, and a sewer hose). The Jon-ny Partner is also compatible with the SCAT Machine. Dry weight is 20 pounds (90 when full). Capacity is 50 to 60 user-days—calculated at 27 cubic inches per person, per day, and based on a study of boaters who ate such things as pork chops and omelets for breakfast! Stout handles at seat level and a square design (12 × 12 × 17 inches) ensure stable seating. The toilet seat has a flange that fits down inside the box and provides additional stability when in use but can require cleaning before packing away. River outfitters catering to high-end clients will sometimes bring enough Jon-ny Partners to open a new one every day. Sells mostly to commercial and private whitewater boaters and to hunting parties for base camps. The Forest Service in Alaska and Idaho packs them in with trail crews. To find on the Partner Steel website: click on MORE, then CAMPSITE. This company also manufactures the **Wishy-Washy Hand Washer** ($123), the ultimate in *sanitary*, because the flow is activated by an in-line foot pump. No grubby fingers on a knob or shut-off valve. Available in *tall* or *short* versions (the latter for placing on a table). Station in both potty and kitchen areas. This is a two-bucket system— supply your own buckets—one for fresh water (not for drinking), the other for soapy wastewater. Don't forget to dispose of the wastewater above the high-water line, or follow local regulations, as in the Grand Canyon.

Jon-ny Partner
www.partnersteel.com
Partner Steel Company
3187 Pole Line Road
Pocatello, ID 83201
✉ camp@partnersteel.com
☎ 208-233-2371

ECO-Safe Ammo Box Toilet System ($229 with traditional seat; $209 with square seat), designed to fit inside a 20 mm surplus ammo can ($49.95), gives double protection against spillage and odor. The tank (17 × 7½ × 13½ inches tall) comes equipped with a 6-inch-diameter screw-top lid; a 3-inch flush-out hole and flexible drain hose; a ½-inch garden-hose-to-box adapter; gasket-sealing plugs; a plug wrench tool; and a choice in toilet-seat assemblies. All fasteners and accessories are made of rustproof materials. Dry weight (tank only) is 5¼ pounds. Accommodates 50 user-days. Sells mostly to commercial and private rafters. **Spare tank** ($129).

The **Boom Box Toilet** ($169) is smaller, with a 2½-gallon tank and self-storing seat. At 13½ × 9 × 8 inches tall, it's the right size for canoes. Comes with the same fittings, hoses, plugs, and wrench as the larger Ammo Box Toilet. Dry weight is 2½ pounds; good for 20 user-days. Has the oddest-looking seat, yet people rave about it—perhaps because it sits so low to the ground, you squat over it.

The ECO-Safe tanks are made of rotomolded "crushproof" high-density polyethylene, with rounded corners for easy cleaning, and a pressure-release vent in the lids. Compatible with RV dumping stations and the SCAT Machine. Pacific River Supply also manufactures the **Clean Mountain Can** (page 63) that's appropriate for individual poop-packers or very small groups.

ECO-Safe Toilet Systems
www.pacificriversupply.com
Pacific River Supply
3675 San Pablo Dam Road
El Sobrante, CA 94803
✉ mike@pacificriversupply.com
☎ 510-223-3675

Coyote Portable Toilet ($194.95) is a wide-based box (12 × 12 × 14 inches tall) of high-density polyethylene, with rounded corners for easy cleaning, though minus a pressure-release valve. Comes with a 10-inch screw-on, gasket-sealed lid; a 3-inch gasket-sealed flush-out plug; an accordion drain hose; a ¾-inch freshwater hose fitting with adapter; a separate raised fiberglass toilet seat; and tie-down webbing. The screw-top lid serves as the seat cover while in camp. Carry by the tie-down webbing or by the lip around the top of the box. **Spare box** ($119.95).

Dry weight, including seat and all components, is 11 pounds; capacity is 60 user-days. Compatible with RV dumping stations and the SCAT Machine. Meets all BLM, NPS, and USFS regulations.

Coyote (Bagless) Portable Toilet
www.riversports.com
Four Corners River Sports
360 South Camino del Rio
Durango, CO 81301
✉ info@riversports.com
☎ 800-426-7637 (toll-free)

D-Can (around $150) is a new—as in, never before employed as a toilet—25 mm surplus ammo can (17½ × 10 × 14½ inches tall), which is 2½ inches wider and more stable than the 20 mm and 1 inch wider than the 30 mm. The accompanying toilet seat has a flat-closing, no-air-gap lid (to keep from attracting flies), and it's mounted on a slide-on aluminum top for using in camp. You'll want to purchase a secondary 20 mm can for storing the seat and potty supplies while on the river. Dry weight is 23 pounds, with a capacity of 70 user-days ("hero use" up to 80). The D-Can is SCAT Machine compatible, or you can purchase an ordinary funnel to use at RV dumping stations and then clean with your own elbow grease. Those interested in purchasing a D-Can are advised to call for the current pricing. Canyon REO also rents D-Cans (see page 53); they specialize in private-trip rental equipment—from rafts to camp kitchens to potties.

D-Can
www.canyonreo.com
Canyon River Equipment
Outfitters
PO Box 3493
Flagstaff, AZ 86003
✉ info@canyonreo.com
☎ 800-637-4604 (toll-free)

Cleanwaste GO Anywhere Portable Toilet ($73.45), used with individual **GO Anywhere Toilet Kits** ($31.45 for 12-pack, each with t.p. and sanitary wipe), has a 14-inch-tall, three-legged frame—making it stable on uneven ground—with a seat like a standard toilet. It will support 500 pounds and folds to the size of a briefcase, with handle. Weighs 7 pounds. The toilet comes with one **Kit**, which is a double-plastic-bagging system, preloaded with **Poo Powder**, a nontoxic proprietary substance. Poo Powder also comes in bulk for extending the use of a bag or using in your own bags. River and horse-packing groups may want to store full bags in a rocket box. Toss the used bags into the regular garbage. A 7-pound **Privacy Shelter** ($146.95) is handy for use right in camp. Find more information on the Kits and Poo Powder, for use without the sit-upon frame, on page 60.

GO Anywhere Portable
Toilet & Toilet Kits
(aka Pett Toilet & Wag Bags)
www.gocleanwaste.com
Cleanwaste
290 Arden Drive
Belgrade, MT 59714
✉ info@gocleanwaste.com
☎ 877-520-0999 (toll-free)

RESTOP Commode ($60.00) is a 5-gallon bucket made of thick-walled, heavy-duty polyethylene that resists becoming brittle and cracking in temperatures of extreme cold or becoming soft in extreme heat. This is *not* the generic 5-gallon paint or pickle bucket—it's been tested by the US Marine Corps with 300 pounds of pressure over 10 hours. Included in the price are a tight-sealing screw-on lid (Gamma Lid) and a washable, flexible foam toilet seat (also sold separately, $19.95). Use with the individual **RESTOP 2** "bag-within-a-bag" system ($3.40; or $81.60 for a case of 24), which contains a proprietary blend of super-absorbent polymers and natural enzymes for disposing of human poop and pee—each comes with a packet of t.p. and a moist antimicrobial wipe. The outer bag is gas-impervious Mylar, for containing odor. Used bags (in line with EPA guidelines) can be tossed into the regular trash. A 7-pound **Privacy Shelter** ($125 in gray; $140 in camouflage) offers seclusion for commode use right in, or near, camp. Find more RESTOP 2 details and instructions for solo-use without the commode on page 61.

The RESTOP commode/bagging system was employed two years in a row on the Eco Everest Expedition (an annual trip organized by Asian Trekking—in conjunction with the programs Cash for Trash and Cleaning Up Everest—that bring down garbage and human waste and try out new eco-equipment). The Canadian distributor is PottiCorp (toll free: 866-325-3865). Although this is a top product and widely approved for most activities, its bucket is not deemed sturdy enough on some

RESTOP
www.restop.com
Restop
2655 Vista Pacific Drive
Oceanside, CA 92056
✉ info@restop.com
☎ 800-366-3941 (toll-free)
☎ 760-741-6600

big-water rivers. Transporting the full bags in ammo cans might be an acceptable solution.

Luggable Loo Toilet Seat and Bucket ($19.95) includes a 5-gallon plastic bucket (gray or camouflage) with a snap-on toilet-seat-with-lid. Or purchase the toilet-seat-with-lid alone ($12.99)—snaps on any 5-gallon utility bucket. **Double Doodie Waste Bags** ($17.95 for 6-pack) are another plastic double-bagging system—these with proprietary Bio-Gel, "similar to what's in baby diapers." The **Hassock Portable Toilet** ($25 to $50) has a t.p. holder and inner removable bucket. Both bucket and hassock are applauded as economical options for *mostly* car/tent camping, because they lack the tight-sealing transport lids needed for activities involving more jouncing around. Use the bags with the commodes or, for backcountry hikers, spread directly on the ground. Widely available in the United States, with prices varying depending on where you buy them. For more discussion on the bags, see page 62.

Luggable Loo and Double Doodie Waste Bags
www.relianceoutdoors.com
Reliance Products
1093 Sherwin Road
Winnipeg, Manitoba
R3H 1A4 Canada
☎ 800-665-0258 (toll-free)

Do-It-Yourself Soil Can

Soil Can ($25 to $35), dreamed up and promoted by Oregon BLM's Kevins (former Kevin McCoy and current Kevin Hoskins), complies with regulations in many backcountry areas.

Gather together a 5-gallon plastic bucket from a hardware store, a Gamma Seal Lid (snap-on ring with screw-on top, fits 12-inch-diameter pails, is leak-proof and easy on the fingernails; find locations on the internet, starting at $7.57), along with a toilet seat and small bag of potting soil. Cheaper yet, beg a bucket from a local deli—green pickle pails were the standard bailing buckets for river rats before the emergence of self-bailing boats. Prime the bucket with 2 inches of potting soil, and after each deposit, throw in another fistful or two. Solids and paper go in the bucket, nothing else. Pee in the bushes well off the river, or in the river, whichever is suggested.

Because the wire handle is the weak link, Hoskins suggests adding a milk crate to your cargo. With cam straps, he secures the crate in a handy place for day access and lashes the bucket inside the crate. Into the crate's nooks, you can tie-in potting soil and other sundries.

Other Hoskins strategies: use the crate in camp as a seat, table, and gear-hauler, and fashion a toilet seat from a foam noodle, slit lengthwise. See also RESTOP's washable foam seat, and for a sturdy, longer-lasting bucket, consider the RESTOP Commode (page 51). Capacity? Well, a party of seven reportedly didn't half-fill a pail in three days. A shorter 2½-gallon bucket is better suited to mini-cats and inflatable kayaks.

All in all, there's nothing better than a Soil Can: it's low cost, lightweight, about the same comfortable height as a home toilet, not yucky to peer into, not odoriferous (adding urine is what produces the knock-you-over smell—although women, by nature, will be adding some pee to the bucket), self-floating if it gets away, and doesn't muck up the inside wall even with jostling. The Soil Can is compatible with the SCAT Machine. If you decide to dump its contents into a vault toilet, then for your ride home, convert the bucket into "Hoskins self-cleaning mode" by pouring in 2 to 3 inches of water and a spritz of disinfectant—chlorine, pine oil, Seventh Generation, whatever your preference. Soil Cans are used by boaters, horse packers, and ATVers.

The other great joy is that Soil Cans are only one step short of being the perfect system—accomplished by composting the contents in your backyard or, perhaps someday, at a small facility near trip's end. Interested? Pick up Joseph Jenkins's splendid volume *The Humanure Handbook: A Guide to Composting Human Manure* (www.josephjenkins.com).

Rentals

D-Can ($3 per day) is a 25 mm surplus ammo can with seat assembly that offers exceptional stability and economy. Also included are a 20 mm can (for storing the seat assembly and potty supplies while on the water) and a "day toilet"—NPS required—consisting of a 50 caliber ammo can with kitty litter. **Wishy-Washy Hand Washer**

stations rent for $35 per trip. Canyon REO specializes in rental gear for private Grand Canyon river trips. They will also deliver to other southwestern rivers, including the San Juan and Salt, and sometimes overland outings. (Actually, they will deliver *anywhere* for a price.) Perfect for people driving through Flagstaff, AZ, coming and going. But here's the best: for a measly $30, at the end of your trip, you're allowed to return a chock-full can to Canyon REO, twirl on your heel and waltz away. (Find a detailed description of the D-Can and contact information on page 50.)

Professional River Outfitters (PRO) rents ($3 per day with a five-day minimum) the traditional World War II 20 mm ammo cans, with a seat assembly to permit holders of noncommercial Grand Canyon river trips. Pick up in Flagstaff, AZ. You receive the ammo can; a toilet seat mounted on a flange that covers the top of the can in camp; a seat riser to keep your keister above the guck; and a storage ammo can. Additional "fill cans" rent for $1 per day. Capacity is 50 deposits. For those already owning 20 mm ammo cans, PRO will sell you the toilet seat mount assembly ($108) and the seat riser ($108). At almost any surplus store, you can purchase a 20 mm ammo can for approximately $40 and be the proud owner of a piece of American history—in fact, several histories. Inspect the gasket to make certain it's in good shape and will be watertight. Bruce Helin, owner of PRO and longtime rafter, recommends marking the cans and lids so "they can be kept together in the same orientation for best sealing." Ammo cans are SCAT Machine compatible. They can be dumped at sewage treatment plants, or buy a funnel and pour the contents down the pipe at an RV dumping station. In the latter two cases, you are stuck with manually cleaning the can. When renting from PRO, the dumping and sterilizing chore is taken, literally, off your hands for as little as $30 per can.

PRO
www.proriver.com
Professional River Outfitters, Inc.
2800 West Route 66
Flagstaff, AZ 86001
✉ info@proriver.com
☎ 800-648-3236 (toll-free)

Since I first began writing about wilderness and human crapola, the practice of packing-it-out has moved from riverbanks, up mountainsides, across deserts, and out onto oceans. The number of people inspired to invent and to adopt poop-removal systems is altogether astounding. Turn the page to "Plight of the Solo Poop-Packer" and find another set of technological advances. I sense we're not far from a marketable sonic Crap-Zapper with the capacity to instantly alter the molecular structure of a human turd. Imagine! A Trekkie phaser gun for the mountain trekker.

Poop and poof!

4
Plight of the Solo Poop-Packer

Everyone, at some time, is a continent of one.
—Pico Iyer, *Falling Off the Map*

You cannot escape. Every day a part of you turns to shit.
—Dan Sabbath and Mandel Hall, *End Product: The First Taboo*

Now for a walk on the wild side. Admittedly, the concept of carting around warm poo in a backpack is not just revolutionary; it is, on initial take, repulsive. To spirit us past the involuntary "gak!" reaction, a kind of higher inspiration is called for. We might try envisioning the whole procedure as one of the marvels of physics—the shrinkage of the food supply as the shit container fills—matter into matter, a perfect example of Einstein's $E = mc^2$. Or we might take heart from Japan's renowned mountaineer, the late Junko Tabei, a woman animated far beyond her small frame. I watched her bound to the podium at the international toilet symposium "Toilets and the Environment" in Toyama, Japan, in 1996. With speech fairly effervescing from every limb of her body, she related her mountaineering experiences, emphasizing the burnished beauty of Antarctica that compelled her not to leave the blot of her own elimination on the scenery. She instead scooped it into a plastic bag, and tied it to the outside of her pack. The package froze, and its to-and-fro thwacking to the rhythm of her gait invigorated her inner sense of being. When a person deals this intimately with her own shit, her soul melds seamlessly with the powers of Nature.

Jim Wilson, another longtime mountaineer—also a writer and the original proprietor of Pipestone Mountaineering in Missoula, Montana—once told me over lunch a story of his own intimacy. I relate it here largely for anyone needing creative power and courage to deal with poop collection. Even the newest products on the market wouldn't have provided much help for Jim, or his climbing partner, also named Jim. In 1997, the two Jims were forging a new route up the east face of Denali. They had reached Harper Glacier, at 16,000 feet (and -40°F), and were aiming for the summit when a storm blew up. Hurrying to pitch their itty-bitty tent next to an offset crevasse for shelter, they crawled in—not knowing they'd be tarrying in such extreme confines for ten days. Without space for much more than sleeping bags, and with the bulk of their gear outside, they managed to eat, hydrate, sleep, and keep up their spirits. The wind ripped 100 to 200 mph; the tent rattled and shuddered. Airborne pebbles off nearby exposed rock sandblasted their walls. It was cold—so cold that if they stepped outside, even in all their clothes, they almost flash-froze.

Then, as it eventually had to, push came to shove, and Wilson thought to line a helmet with a plastic bag. That his helmet was the only one in the tent was his first surprise. Worse, because a helmet's shape is inherently round and the Jims didn't dare make any messy mistakes, everything got up-close and personal fast—each one holding the helmet for the other. The easy part turned out to be abiding by the approved (then) glacial disposal: crack open the tent flap and lob the bag into the crevasse. Two determined Jims made it to the summit. Descending on the standard route, they were able to bum food. But still, Wilson lost fifty pounds in forty-five days and required a six-month recovery.

Wilson's generosity in sharing this humiliating story and agreeing to my printing it turns me shamefaced at the thought of complaining a smidgeon, ever, about tending to my own shit. (Lunch, by the way, during all this, was remarkably tasty!)

As demand escalated for viable, inoffensive methods to transport an individual's fecal matter down from snowy mountaintops, out to trailheads, or off island beaches—lo!—inventive minds went quietly to work, offering aid to solitary poop-packers. We've come a long way now with containers, attitudes, and stoutness of hearts. To keep urging us toward new peaks of genius, here follows a discussion of specifics for optimum solo containers.

A user-friendly solo system has to cover much the same territory as a group's, but designers must take into consideration that the average, hands-on poop-packer might be more of a twice-a-year sojourner, soft on flush apparatus, and, in the beginning, more fastidious than, say, the full-time river guide who's become thoroughly inured to outdoor doodies . . . er, *duties*. To start off, a collection container should be sturdy but lightweight, small enough to be convincingly carried, yet large enough to hold several deposits. It must have a positively reliable seal; no one wants to think about leakage. A shape convenient for direct deposit would be helpful and, when in use, it shouldn't be inclined to tip over. Lovely would be a pressure-release vent to rule out its blowing up. And inexpensive, we'd naturally all appreciate. So we're talking either a reusable container—or an item that's painless to flush and clean—or an item that's completely biodegradable. (Bear in mind that when a plastic bag is promoted as "biodegradable," the term is unregulated with regard to the percentage of actually biodegradable components and the time required to fully degrade.) Other pluses would be compatibility with RV dumping stations, trailhead vault toilets, or septic tanks—and, I'm going to venture to add here, trailhead composting stations. Altogether, solo systems are a tricky bill to fill.

Dismissing, for the time being, the zanier ideas: toting around your own dung-devouring scarab beetles, inventing an energy-bar-sized solar incinerator, or pinning your hopes on a big brother to the world's largest carnivorous plant (the giant montane pitcher plant of Borneo that reportedly likes to dine on shrew poo), we'll move on to considering the known whens and hows of packing-it-out—that is, for all sorts of outdoor-goers in high-use areas in an effort to keep those places sanitary and looking pristine; for sea kayakers, river runners, and cavers, or anyone visiting fragile ecosystems; for all the untidy Himalayan litterbugs; and for rock climbers (long, those uncouth beasts! who *are* mercifully evolving). Understandably, rock climbers have a tough time, given the added acrobatics involved in keeping the face of a mountain clean. What can I say? Practice. Select a mode and hang off the backyard tree.

Solo Poop-Packer Systems

Cleanwaste GO Anywhere Toilet Kit ($31.45 for 12-pack) is a lightweight double-plastic-bagging system. The larger deposit bag is preloaded with Poo Powder; the other is the zip-closing transport bag. Each kit has a packet of toilet paper and a hand-wipe. The deposit bag is generous enough to spread out on the ground and, as my friend Nancy the Caver says, "not have to worry about aim." Its Poo Powder is a nontoxic, proprietary blend that includes a "NASA-developed gelling agent"; it has no smell in itself, but serves to control odor and begin the breakdown of fecal matter. Each deposit bag contains enough powder to solidify 24 to 32 ounces (needs liquid to activate), making it multiple-use. Additional bulk **Poo Powder** ($35.65 for 55 scoops, measuring scoop included; also comes in quantities up to 5 gallons) will extend the use of a bag. The **Pee-Wee** ($19.94 for 12-pack) is a unisex urine bag with Poo Powder that gels 24 ounces of liquid. Used by adults or children when "plumbing's not available." When finished, snap the collar closed. Toss all used bags in the regular garbage (according to EPA guidelines). GO Anywheres provide a sanitary approach for dozens of activities—hiking, boating, cycling, hunting, horse packing—as well as for the military, long-haul truckers, hospitals, and FEMA.

With the GO Anywheres in such wide use, they rate further discussion, particularly for backpackers. Joshua Cole, former Outward Bound program director in Washington state, would tell his student hikers, "Don't tie the bag on the outside of your pack, where it can get poked by a branch or pecked by a bird." One of his groups, while taking a day hike, cached their GO Anywheres in the snow and returned to find "a murder of crows" upon them. Cole recommends tucking a laden bag inside the top of your pack, where it won't get squashed by gear, and then definitely remembering when you take

GO Anywhere Toilet Kit
(aka Wag Bag)
www.gocleanwaste.com
Cleanwaste
1700 Amsterdam Road
Belgrade, MT 59714
✉ info@gocleanwaste.com
☎ 877-520-0999 (toll-free)
☎ 406-388-5999

a break not to sit on that end. Bags will pop by force, he says, but if you're careful, they work "really well." Expect some odor.

RESTOP 2 ($3.40 each; $81.60 for 24-pack) is a patented "bag-within-a-bag" system pre-seeded with a proprietary blend of polymers and enzymes that gels, deodorizes, and biodegrades human waste. Each kit comes with a packet of toilet paper and a moist antimicrobial wipe. The ziplocking transport bag is made of gas-impervious aluminized Mylar—for odor control. Attached is an amply sized plastic bag with its bottom opening into the transport bag. Spread it directly on the ground and make your deposit in the plastic portion. Then lift it by the black plastic drawstrings and give it a quick up-down shake—this motion serves to slide your deposit on down into the silvery bag where the slightly floral-smelling powder resides. Gently squeeze out the air, cinch it up, roll everything into the transport bag, and zip closed. Though it's meant to be a one-use bag, there's enough powder to process "more waste than you could possibly cram in the bag"—reportedly 4 to 5 uses. Pitch laden RESTOP 2 bags (in line with EPA guidelines) in the regular trash. The **RESTOP 1** ($7 for 3 bags and tissues) is a disposable unisex urine bag equipped with a one-way valve to prevent spillage, a plastic collar with a pop-open tab that becomes a handle, and enough proprietary blend to gel 20 ounces of pee. The **RESTOP 2W** ($16 for tote and 5 RS2s) is a plastic mesh tote bag, an easy means to "pack it in, pack it out." The **RESTOP Commode**, an amazingly tough 5-gallon bucket, is discussed on page 51.

RESTOP
www.restop.com
RESTOP
2655 Vista Pacific Drive
Oceanside, CA 92056
✉ info@restop.com
☎ 800-366-3941 (toll-free)
☎ or 760-741-6600

Biffy Bag—also called the "pocket potty" or "biffy in a jiffy"—($3.49 each; $9.99 for 3-pack; $31.99 for 10-pack; also sold in larger quantities) is another two-bag system but with three layers, decidedly different user positioning, and you are in charge of adding the supplied seeding. Each comes with a packet of Biffy Powder, toilet paper, and an oversize hand-wipe. The ziplocking

transport bag is made of gas-impervious, odor-controlling aluminized Mylar, lined with black plastic. The attached green plastic bag
has a narrowing rounded bottom that facilitates bringing deposited
poop into contact with the waste treatment powder. The proprietary Biffy Powder (with enzymes and a decay catalyst) is said to
actively foam up around the deposit, immediately sealing a layer
on the top, while engulfing and neutralizing waste and odors, then
solidify from the top down. Designed for one use (for sanitary
purposes) but reports have it that bags have been employed for as
many as four poops. Contains enough powder to take care of four,
but to ensure complete solidification you might want to order more
Biffy Powder ($4.99 for 4-pack). To use, open the silvery bag,
pull out the inner green bag, and dump in the Biffy Powder. Tear
the green bag's two tabs along their perforations—turning them
into straps that tie around your waist—and having dropped your
drawers by now, clamp the bag onto your, so to speak, poop deck.
Then, reach between your legs, tug the bag forward, and bending
your knees slightly, go for it. Can also be used with a commode, if
you prefer to sit. This system has been tested six ways to Sunday
and touts a burst-strength rating of 50 psi, a puncture-resistance
rating of 13 psi, and 4,000 times
the odor containment of a standard
garbage bag. A loaded one survived
a 20-foot drop onto pavement.
The Biffy Bag is a proud partner
of the Leave No Trace Center for
Outdoor Ethics and conforms to
EPA guidelines.

Biffy Bag
www.biffybag.com
LEDO Environmental, LLC
3535 North View Lane
Woodbury, MN 55125
✉ info@biffybag.com
☎ 651-206-3078

Double Doodie Waste Bags with Bio-Gel ($17.95 for 6-pack) is
another double-bagging system, this time with proprietary Bio-Gel.
You can purchase the bags with or
without the Bio-Gel, so check what
you're getting. (Double Doodie
Plus Bags always come with Bio-
Gel.) Use in a campground with
one of the Reliance commodes (see
page 52), or in the backcountry,

Double Doodie Waste Bags
www.relianceoutdoors.com
Reliance Products
1093 Sherwin Road
Winnipeg, Manitoba
R3H 1A4 Canada
☎ 800-665-0258 (toll-free)

directly on the ground. Provide your own toilet paper and hand-washing arrangement.

Clean Mountain Can ($69.95) is a straight-sided barrel (9-inch diameter × 11-inch height; 2.2 pounds) of high-density poly-ethylene, sturdy enough for civilized sitting-upon, aided by the 8-inch-diameter hole with 1-inch flange. CMCs are equipped with a Gortex gas-release vent, a screw-type lid, and a webbing har-ness for both locking down the lid and strapping the affair onto a pack, and also, I'd say, to a sled, raft, canoe, mule, or for road trips back-of-beyond. Capacity is 14 to 20 *climber* user-days . . . meaning climbers are undergoing rigorous physical activity and don't eat quite like curled-up fireside readers.

Alaska mountaineering ranger Roger Robinson first conceived of the CMC, and Denali Climbing Rangers endorsed them. Denali National Park then purchased 1,100 CMCs for circulation and arranged for a dumping and cleaning service, all funded, in part, by a portion of climbers' special-use fees. Removing human waste from Denali's high camp at 17,200 feet has been required since 2006, while other areas still allowed deep-crevasse disposal. Now, with multiyear research studies showing that fecal pathogens are resurfacing down-glacier and in waterways, the crevasse disposal will likely change, with additional areas regulated for packing-it-out. CMCs were used by the Eco Everest Expedition. And Kiliwarriors, a largely Maasai outfitter for Kilimanjaro climbs, began valiantly removing excrement from the overnight Crater Camp in 2004, using CMCs. Kiliwarriors is passionate about preserving cleanli-ness and reducing waste on Kilimanjaro. A privately owned CMC can be dumped at a sewage treatment plant, RV dumping station, or trailhead vault toilet. Wash at home with soap and water. Lining your can with a GO Anywhere bag and adding more Poo Powder simplifies cleanup, but be sure the bag ends up in the regular trash. Purchase a CMC through Pacific River Supply or Decker's Hot Camp Showers in Petaluma, CA (hotcampshowers.com).

Clean Mountain Can (CMC)
www.pacificriversupply.com
Pacific River Supply
3675 San Pablo Dam Road
El Sobrante, CA 94803
✉ mike@pacificriversupply.com
☎ 510-223-3675

Big Wall Can ($79) is Mountain Tools' adaptation of the Clean Mountain Can with a different webbing harness, for hauling. Stacks right under a climber's haul bag. "Because nature doesn't necessarily schedule her calls for convenient locations"—it's not so easy to sit on a swinging can—extreme climbers do their number twos in a brown paper bag, then roll it up and tuck it into the can. Prerigging the paper bags with a bit of kitty litter is recommended. BWCs can be dumped in the same places as CMCs. If lining with a Go Anywhere, deposit the bag in the regular garbage. Larry Arthur, owner of Mountain Tools, promotes BWCs for expedition outfitters, tour operators, outdoor instructors, and firefighters in countries around the world. He will ship anywhere, including to General Delivery (say, at Yosemite) to accommodate traveling climbers.

Big Wall Can (BWC)
www.mtntools.com
Mountain Tools
PO Box 222295
Carmel, CA 93922
✉ On the website, click on "ask the tool man."
☎ 800-510-2514 (toll-free); for tech questions: 831-620-0911

> **Bagging Alerts:** Because the various proprietary "magic" powders may need to be activated by liquid, if you're not also peeing in the bag, pour in ½ to 1 ounce of something like water, coffee . . . beer? Do NOT drop anything bagged into vault toilets or septic systems. Garbage cans, oddly enough, are where they belong. None of the current "biodegradable" plastic bagging, or even double bagging, will completely contain odors. The ziplocking aluminized Mylar bags handle the odor well, but are even farther from biodegradable. As for reopening these bags and spreading them out for additional deposits—I know that sane and normal people do this, but—it's difficult!

Shhh-it! Kit (3-inch-diameter × 12-inch length; 0.62 pounds; $39) is an exceptionally lightweight, washable-reusable, personal container. The aluminum cylinder can be custom cut to any length your heart desires—and signed, if you wish! It's equipped with rubber-gasketed screw-on lids at both ends and holds 2 to 4 deposits with corresponding t.p.(depending, of course, on a person's intake; do you eat like a butterfly, a pink flamingo, or a wild boar?). Has no pressure-release vent but, during testing, a packed tube, under two days of direct California sun, never blew a lid. The Shhh-it! Kit can be tucked inside a backpack, pannier, saddle bag, or dry bag, along with a plastic bag containing supplies of t.p., paper wraps, and hand sanitizer, or slip everything into the special **SK Ditty Bag** ($15) and secure anywhere with attaching straps. Deposits are made simply, and almost anywhere, onto a couple squares of absorbent paper (unbleached paper toweling is recommended; make certain it's the kind that holds together when wet—test first at home with water). Wrap your leaving like a burrito and slip it into the cylinder. In seriously wet or snowy conditions, for insurance, spread out a piece of wax paper first. The SK has no plastic bags to worry about biodegrading, perforating, or plugging up the honey wagon's pump; no poo powder to spill; no smell; no flies. Empty the cylinder into a campground vault toilet. To push your packages on through, remove both lids. Carry some sort of utensil in a plastic bag in your vehicle: for instance, a long-handled kitchen spoon or spatula (not wooden), bent with pliers to handy angles. I use a whisk, with a clump of t.p. in front of it. Unless you've been stricken with trekker's trots—then all bets are off—your burritos are tidy little packages that pop right out. Clean at home with a bottle brush reserved solely for this purpose and kept alongside your home toilet bowl brush. After washing with soap and water (no lousy threads on the inside to make life difficult), leave the tool and kit in your vehicle. The Shhh-it! Kit is a great option for the extra adventurous and those wanting to go no-frills, reusable, and ecological.

Shhh-it! Kit
www.kathleeninthewoods.net
PO Box 342
Victor, MT 59875
✉ Email off the website
(Check with Kathleen to see if this product has found start-up funding and gone into production.)

Do-It-Yourself, Etc.

Poop Tubes (made of 4-inch-diameter, 12-inch-long PVC pipe; 2.3 pounds; $15 to $20 for parts, minus glue) first arrived in the high Sierras around 2000, via Mark Butler, a climber and physical science specialist with the NPS. He declined any claims on the tube's design but he used one, promoted them as inexpensive make-at-home containers for packing-it-out, and advocated their use on the climbing routes in Yosemite National Park. Bingo! An end to flinging laden paper bags into thin air. Assembly is easy from materials available in hardware and plumbing stores. Simply cut a piece of white PVC pipe to the length of your trip, so to speak—10 to 20 inches. Glue a cap on one end and a slip/thread coupling for a screw plug on the other (see illustration). With super tape (climber's webbing) and a little duct tape, sling the tube from the bottom of your haul sack. Make deposits in brown paper bags seeded with kitty litter and stuff into the tube. At the end of the trip, the contents are dumped into a Park vault toilet.

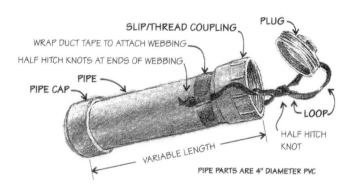

SLIP/THREAD COUPLING
PLUG
WRAP DUCT TAPE TO ATTACH WEBBING
HALF HITCH KNOTS AT ENDS OF WEBBING
PIPE
PIPE CAP
LOOP
HALF HITCH KNOT
VARIABLE LENGTH
PIPE PARTS ARE 4" DIAMETER PVC

For the adventurer willing to leave behind Western civilization's characteristic prudishness, there are more homegrown ways of coping, and I don't mean enemas or the untraceable rumor of biodegradable bags made of cheese. Inexpensive household containers have been appropriated for outdoor use on many occasions. I have reports of plastic snap-lid salad bowls servicing backpackers, two people to a bowl in some cases. (I can't help wondering whether this type of sharing can cement relationships in the same way drought-induced showering together does.) One flaw in this system involves methane buildup: a morning's hike under a hot sun will invariably pop the seal. But people seem to manage by being attentive. Karen Stimpson, as trail keeper for the Maine Island Trail, once revealed that a bowl of similar design was her favorite. She started out with the kitty litter routine, but progressed to rolling her deposit in a bit of sand, earth, or dried leaves before scooping it up. "The container cleans easier," she said. Surely this is all new testimony to the function of salad bowls. A note on kitty litter: buy the cheapest available; it's usually straight bentonite, a powdery clay soil.

If you lack a good relationship with gravity, like me, here's a tip for solitary collecting in a snowscape. Scoop out a depression and tuck your container into it. With leisure and inclination, you can build a royal throne, a chair-high mound with a container hole in the seat. Too cold to plunk right down? Carefully, rest your buns upon your gloves.

The Much-Needed Demise of Frosting

In the 1990s, a wild form of backcountry human waste disposal suddenly appeared—termed, in different parts of the country, as "frosting" or "smearing." The activity became cause for a great deal of mirth in this book's second edition. A sort of "Let's all go frost a rock!" But it didn't take long for prevailing thinking on this to change, and for a number of good reasons.

Beyond the obvious—that most anywhere human excrement is left exposed, insects and animals swiftly arrive—we know now from actual field studies that microorganisms in fecal smears, even under close to optimal conditions and technique, can persist a lot longer than originally assumed—as can the feces themselves. Gratitude here goes to the Leave No Trace Center for Outdoor Ethics, the National Park Service, the National Outdoor Leadership School, and Ferris State University for undertaking a series of field studies on the fate of feces and fecal microorganisms in samples of varying thickness at locations in three different environments—arid, temperate, and alpine. The sites were chosen in Mount Rainier National Park and the Wenatchee National Forest.

The long of it: Someone likely offered up a lovely specimen and others donned protective gloves. Smears were set up inside wire cages, for keeping out animals, and then elaborate monitoring took place over a period of months, with varied results. The short of it: Insects at one location arrived within fifteen minutes and insect larvae at another was evident on day two; smears at some locations began to desiccate in short order; but fecal organisms at other sites were found still surviving at four and a half months. Because the testing was limited to *bacteria,* the staying power of viruses, protozoa, and helminths (or worms) was not included.

Add the findings of these studies to other more casual observations of smearing and an axiom arises: Optimal smearing is not something often accomplished. Adult humans, come to find out, aren't terribly talented at fecal artistry. Some instead were— chickening out?—leaving plain piles in the open or whipping up lumpy mashed-potato-like toppings, rather than painstakingly smushing to the required paper-thin veneer. Top considerations, ultimately, must go to our cherished waterways and wildlife, as well as others of our own species, all of which stand vulnerable to raw human feces. Thus, the very outdoor schools that first adopted frosting are no longer promoting it. **And I'm not promoting it.** Packing-it-out is far superior in all but *extremely* select situations. I describe the method here and underline the severe cautions, because to ignore the whole topic—in the hope that someone who barely grasps its outline is not roaming the mountains, experimenting—is foolish.

Frosting is not a matter for the timid or the tyro and demands a well-schooled background in meteorology, climate, and terrain. Four elements MUST be present: an extremely remote location, intense sunlight, a dry landscape, and scant soil (that is, no bacterial activity or limited soil depth). This presumes the location is above timberline or nearly so, or in a blazing desert or extensive boulder field. If not a dry climate, it must be a long, dry season with no chance of fecal matter being carried away by storm runoff or buried beneath snowdrifts to thaw in the spring. Remoteness is a huge criteria, so as not to ruin the next person's well-deserved sojourn through scenic grandeur—the site should not see another soul for six months. In effect, the sewage treatment plant of the heavens, our almighty solar incinerator must be at work: ultraviolet rays scorching the life out of pathogens and dehydrating the leaving until the wind carries off the final parched flakes.

Now for procedure. Because sunbeams are the prime factor in desiccation, the selected spot must catch daylong direct rays. A handy stone serves as a spatula. After shitting atop the rock, spread the leaving as thinly as possible, then prop the stone alongside, turned up to the sun. I once asked, "Just how thin are we talking here?" The answer came, "Pretend you're frosting a cake." As it turns out, even that's too thick; a correct simile is "like rolling paint onto a wall." If midway through, your mind comes unstuck, don't UNDER ANY CIRCUMSTANCES give up and go home. A person's continued efforts, at this point, must be outright, absolute, sine qua non . . . in pursuit of another miracle in the long string given us by the sun gods, Helios and Apollo.

Our wildlands shrink. Our urban lifestyles make for more madness. Our longing to touch nature waxes. More high use of cherished lands is directly ahead. Simple arithmetic tells us that fewer one-sit holes and more packing-it-out will allow increased visitation. In essence, ballooning backcountry population and disappearing wilderness translate into more crap in your pack! Something to remember next time your vote is needed for wildland preservation.

So off we go, wending Earth's curves from her craggy rock faces to her seashore marshes, all in the company of jolly good friends, with only one act likely remaining solitary—that of shitting. Yet take comfort. You won't, in fact, be alone—in either the queasiness or the shared virtue. Trust me, individual porta looing is nearly a backwoods tsunami. Don't be a laggard. Grab your container. Bring your clothespin, if it helps. And take those little piles with you when you leave.

5
Trekker's Trots

Lomotil, Lomotil, wherefore art thou, my Lomotil?
—Anonymous traveler in Puerto Vallarta

During the violent shaking of an earthquake, a solid, earth-filled dam can turn to liquid and wash away. Trekker's trots is a similar phenomenon occurring within the intestinal walls of the mammalian body. I've seen it happen to my Clydesdales during Fourth of July fireworks at the county fair. Seconds after the first cannon blasts, the horses are dispersing streams of green alfalfa soup. When this instantaneous liquefaction happens in the species *Homo sapiens*, we call it *turista, trekker's trots, Montezuma's revenge, the green-apple two-step*, or, quite simply, *the shits*.

Such a watery biological response can be brought about by any number of things, but especially travel. Our immune systems grow up where we do, leaving our resistance unequipped for various foreign foods and water. Sojourning can be overwhelming; changes in climate, altitude, and time zone all take their toll on the human system. Anxiety about making all (or missing half) your travel connections can have you reaching for Kaopectate. The sheer fright of an adventure a bit too thrilling can "set it off" faster than a shaken beer exiting its bottle. Two of my favorite friends—mother and daughter—are often assailed by this disorder when they set foot in an airport; thus, they've coined another modern euphemism, *airporters*.

This short chapter—short, as I hope all your bouts with this subject will be—emphasizes prevention. Once you've been struck by an airporter, there isn't a whole lot to be said—only to resist cleaning up in a nearby creek and remember to do any washing above the high-water line. It helps to have a trusted friend to bring you wash water and clothes and offer comfort—someone who won't hold their sides in uproarious laughter.

Zeroing in on prevention brings us straight to sanitation practices. Enteric pathogens (the intestinal bad guys) are transmitted through forms of fecal-oral contact, so, logically, the first step toward protection is to ritualize handwashing. Spur yourself and all your traveling companions into the habit of washing *after* squatting and *before* preparing food or eating. Be neurotic about it! The importance of handwashing can't be stressed enough for outdoor folks who tend to equate ruggedness—that messing and sweating about in earth's fresh, fragrant dirt—with the *primeval*, that long-sought-after excuse not to bathe for days. At group campsites, near the communal loo, station biodegradable soap along with a spigoted water container or a hanging reservoir with a shut-off clamp—even more sanitary is a **Wishy Washy Hand Washer** station, with foot-pump activation (see www.partnersteel.com or page 48). And throughout the day, keep a bottle of hand sanitizer within reach. Also included under prevention is the practice of watching closely what you eat and drink. Properly refrigerate perishable foods and carefully disinfect all water for drinking, cooking, food washing, and dishwashing.

Other guidebooks extensively cover food matters, while here, I want to focus on the off-road issues of field water disinfection, the treatment of backcountry water for infectious organisms. In view of rapidly changing product lines and prices, as well as today's far-reaching internet access and the convenience of comparison print-outs in outdoor stores, what follows is my offering of a few good gear-review links and a general discussion. With this overview, you'll have a head start on the dizzying dozens of *disinfecting* systems.

www.cleverhiker.com

www.sectionhiker.com

www.trailspace.com

First, let's clear up a few terms, with the help of Dr. Howard D. Backer, MD, an avid outdoorsman and author of the forty-odd pages on field water treatment in the weighty book *Wilderness Medicine* (5th edition) by Paul S. Auerbach (St. Louis, MO: C.V. Mosby Company, 2007). A two-volume e-book edition (Amsterdam, Netherlands: Elsevier, 2017) is now also available.

For more than a quarter century, Dr. Backer has been known as the "genius and authority" on the subject of field water treatment. He tells us that *disinfection* means "removing or destroying harmful microorganisms," and should not be confused with *sterilization*, "the destruction or removal of all life forms," which is "not necessary, since not all organisms are enteric human pathogens." (This is not to infer that the processes that do kill everything are to be dismissed.) *Purification* is another term that shows up in product promotional literature. Backer calls purification, technically, "the removal of organic or inorganic chemicals and particulate matter, including radioactive particles." Although "purification can eliminate offensive color, taste, and odor, it may not remove or kill microorganisms." That said, there are some purification systems that manage to accomplish all they claim to.

Enteric Pathogens

The intestinal waterborne troublemakers afflicting humans come in three sizes. Listed in descending order, they are **parasitic organisms, bacteria,** and **viruses (P, B, and V). Remember these!** The first of the three, and largest, are the protozoan cysts of *Giardia* and the oocysts of *Cryptosporidium* (you won't see them swimming, it's not like studying polliwogs). As discussed in chapter 2, they are widespread in wilderness water and must be considered a potential hazard everywhere in the world. The bacteria that are problematic cannot be called epidemic in the backcountry of the US, Canada, or the UK, but *E. coli* and *Salmonella* do turn up and are seemingly on the increase. If you're traveling to developing countries where sanitation is poor and municipal water supplies (even hotel water) are suspect, you will need further protection from waterborne viruses, such as *Norovirus* and *Hepatitis A*.

Mechanical Field Water Filtration Systems

Mechanical systems can effectively strain out protozoan cysts and, to varying degrees, block bacteria. The devices do this by trapping P and B in their internal elements or cartridges, built from a variety of materials—including ceramic, silica, pleated glass fibers, and hollow plastic fibers. Operation is by means of hand-pumping, squeezing, sipping, sucking, or a drip gravity-feed. A filter with an "absolute" pore size of 3.0 microns will remove the microorganisms of *Giardia* and *Cryptosporidium*; a filter of 0.2 microns will eliminate all bacteria ("absolute" means that no organism bigger than that size can pass through).

Note: The EPA does NOT "approve" or "endorse" any field water filtration apparatus as such, but they do offer guidelines and many products conform to these. When you see packages displaying an EPA registration number, it merely means they have been registered as a pesticide (as in iodine) and tested and found not to cause "harmful health effects." Without government-regulated testing, the best we can do is to rely on reputable companies. Do resist buying from Amazon (they're largely what's wrong with this world); instead, support local mom-and-pop shops and buy direct from trustworthy product manufacturers.

The life of a filter (given usually in liter or gallon capacity) and a system's flow rate (how fast you can fill your water bottle or reservoir) will fluctuate drastically downward when you're drawing from muddy, debris-laden, or glacial water; when your apparatus, over time, begins to clog; or when some Sasquatch plants a big foot on your hose.

Prefilters are for capturing the larger crud and sediment. You can also prefilter the prefilter, using cheesecloth, pantyhose, a bandana, or coffee filters, or by letting the water sit for a while to settle out. Some pumps are designed to unclog by back-flushing (during field maintenance); others are cleaned by scrubbing the element's surface; still others cannot be cleaned and need replacements.

With any filter, examine the housing regularly for cracks that might admit contamination. Become familiar with the cost of replacement filters, because eventually they all need to be replaced. Ceramic filters are initially expensive, but they last the longest and are easily cleaned with the light touch of a brush or pan-scrubbing pad. And be aware that freezing ruins hollow-fiber filters, except for . . . the MSR Guardian Purifier (read on).

Activated carbon filters come integrated with other filters or as add-ons. They remove organic chemicals such as herbicides, pesticides, diesel fuel, solvents, and fertilizers, as well as iodine you might be using to kill viruses—thus, offering better health and better taste. On the downside, carbon filters require frequent replacement, regardless of whether they're clogged. They collect material by the process of *adsorption* (the clinging of molecules to a solid surface), and when surface limits are reached, previously adsorbed materials begin to dislodge. Some companies contend their cartridges will (helpfully) clog well before capacity of the activated carbon is used up.

It is an advantage to have a pump that dismantles handily for field maintenance and cleaning (don't forget to carry spare parts and necessary tools). Some models demand the skill of an arthroscopic surgeon; ask for a demonstration or watch an online video. Keep in mind that the perfect filter does not exist—there are always trade-offs—and no filter will give you 100 percent protection (although close).

Other things to consider are price, weight, durability, ease of pumping, flow rate, adequate length of hoses, your group's size, and the duration of your trip. Let's not forget accessories: lid adapters for direct pumping into your favorite trail bottle; tote bags; a showerhead attachment for a hanging reservoir; and, in some cases, prefilters and carbon filters.

Avoiding Viruses

Now for those deadly little guys, viruses, and a look at some applications that, when properly executed, are capable of eliminating P, B, and V in one fell swoop. A mechanical filtration system with a pore size fine enough to strain out viruses will make driving water through it impossible. (In general, the smaller the pore size, the harder the pumping.) So, to knock out viruses, we turn elsewhere.

Boiling is the tried-and-true method from earlier days, when people were few and firewood was plentiful, and it's always an option for killing all waterborne enteric pathogens immediately. From Dr. Backer again: "Any water is adequately disinfected by the time it reaches the boiling point [let's call it a rolling boil]—even at altitudes of 24,000 feet where the boiling point is as low as 74.5°C [166.1°F]." But the CDC, EPA, and others, according to Backer, recommend a one-minute boil for added safety, and at higher elevations, make that three minutes. The major drawback—in our age of Leave No Trace ethics and not wanting to break branches off all the trees bordering a campsite—is dragging around enough fuel to do the job.

Steripen from Katadyn (3 to 6 ounces; $65 to $110) offers various sterilizers that work by means of ultraviolet light, killing P, B, and V in almost a flash, by altering the DNA of microorganisms so they cannot reproduce. These little magic wands are divine for anyone who loathes pumping. They are good for high-country backpackers and also international city trekkers (eliminating the constant purchase of bottled water). Steripens, however, require batteries. They accept several kinds (some USB-port rechargeable), purifying 20 to 150 liters. The lamp life is 8,000 uses—if you reach that number, you're promised a new one, free. They all come with a neoprene pouch, and one has a prefilter. On the problem end: they're delicate, mostly useless on murky water, finicky in freezing temperatures, and don't filter out chemicals. If you spring for one, treat it gingerly and perhaps plan time for prewarming in your armpit and for prefiltering silt and floaties.

Mountain Safety Research (MSR) Guardian Purifier (1 pound and 1 ounce; $349.95) is a "mechanical virus-filtration pump"—just after I told you there's no such thing! This product emerged from medical and military circles. Its "leading-edge" filter with hollow fibers—and teensy-weensy pores—filters out P, B, and V and works only because it back-flushes (self-cleans) with every stroke. Touted as "durable" when dropped on cement. Withstands freezing—if you empty it thoroughly—which means you don't have to cuddle it all night. It can handle filthy water (attached prefilter helps with larger debris), and treats up to 10,000 liters per cartridge at an easy and speedy 2.5 liters per minute. Field maintenance is simple: an occasional rinsing of the pressure relief valve. The only thing the GP doesn't do is eliminate chemicals (see "activated carbon filters" on page 75). The price is high but so is the appreciation.

LifeStraw Mission is a gravity-feed setup for camp that filters P, B, V, *and* microplastics. It has a long life and is compact but seemingly has a number of quirks. I refer you to the review on www.trailspace.com.

Grayl Ultralight, with its interesting technology, takes care of P, B, V, *and* nasty chemicals. It's inexpensive but has limited capacity. See the review on www.sectionhiker.com.

Halogen chemical disinfectants, **chlorine** and **iodine**, are inexpensive, small in bulk, and lightweight. Chlorine has long been the preferred disinfectant for municipal water supplies, and iodine has been used by the military since the beginning of the 1900s. Although halogens work well on B and V, the Ps have a resistance to them. *Cryptosporidium,* in particular, is highly resistant to chlorine. Plan on waiting the allotted time—up to four hours, or more—or using, additionally, a mechanical filter for protozoa before (or after) halogenating. Halogens will not disinfect adequately when prepared in insufficient concentrations or without suitable contact time. High pH, colder water temperatures, and cloudy water all decrease effectiveness.

Chlorine-dioxide tablets are safer to use than household liquid bleach. Iodine is available in tablets, crystals, and tincture. Because the stability of tablets is sometimes questionable and they are inexpensive, always buy a new supply before each trip and keep them out of the heat. You must be mindful of the corrosive effects of halogens, especially of carelessly handled iodine crystals. And yet, **Polar Pure** (5 ounces; about $20) is a bottle of iodine crystals with a neat little trap to safely contain them. A thermometer on the side of the bottle tells you what the dosage should be. The crystals are long-lasting and not affected by age or exposure to air. A bottle treats up to 2,000 liters (though it's marketed as killing only B and V). The use of iodine warrants some medical warnings: **do not take when pregnant, or if you**

have iodine sensitivity or a history (including family history) of thyroid disease.

Additional worthwhile devices include the classic **Katadyn Pocket Filter** (19 ounces, $369.95) with a silver-impregnated ceramic filter that removes P and B and is easily field cleaned. Pricey, yes, but it's been around for half a century and comes with a stunning twenty-year guarantee, soon balancing the cost of frequent replacement cartridges for the less expensive pumps. Katadyn also has **hanging gravity-feed reservoirs**—no pumping involved. A bigger draw for me are **attachable showerheads**. Find them at both Katadyn (retail in various outdoor stores) and MSR.

In the final analysis, choose a system that fits your lifestyle and destinations. Are you a zealous day hiker, a mountain peak to pinnacle maniac, or off to the Amazon in a dugout? Safe drinking water is serious business. Approach with caution any products ringing of fads or resembling toys. Read the fine print, ask questions, feel satisfied. In Montana, I find the local outdoor-store folks well versed in equipment—they are party to all the raves and complaints—and over the top in friendliness.

A wise idea: whichever device you eventually select, carry a convenient backup system (maybe a LifeStraw, Steripen, or halogen).

Some hunerd—it seems—years ago on trips to Mexico, I clutched my prescription bottle of tiny Lomotil tablets with the preoccupation of a small child's death grip on her teddy bear. In those days, Lomotil was all that a general practitioner knew to recommend. These days, you can buy Imodium over-the-counter and travel medicine has become a specialty, called *emporiatrics*. A network of travel clinics strung around the country offers informational handouts, provides pre-trip immunizations, suggests appropriate prophylactic medications, and diagnoses post-trip ailments (most people will be home by the time *Giardia* symptoms first appear).

Prophylactic drugs for a mild case of *turista* are generally not advised for healthy travelers because the medication can get in the way of diagnosis and treatment if you contract something more serious. The exception to this is Pepto-Bismol, which is both a light preventive and a cure. Consult your health care provider prior to foreign travel about using Pepto-Bismol.

Staying Hydrated

If, after all this, trekker's trots happens to get you, it's critical to maintain your hydration. Oral hydration can usually be accomplished with glasses of water and those little ORT (oral rehydration therapy) packets from the World Health Organization (http://www.rehydrate.org/solutions/packaged.htm), as long as you, of course, remember to pack them. Otherwise, **drink alternate 8-ounce glasses of:**

1. Orange, apple, or any fruit juice rich in potassium with a teaspoon of honey and a pinch of salt. (For me, the taste of salt in fruit juice triggers an automatic gag reflex; instead, I fall back on the old tequila routine—lick the salt from my hand, chug the juice.)
2. Water, with a teaspoon of baking soda as a buffer for stomach acid.

If nothing else, down some salt and a Coke. Diarrhea combined with vomiting can create a life-threatening loss of body fluid. If you can't keep down rehydration drinks—particularly in a hot climate—seek medical attention and intravenous fluids.

While we're on the subject of remembering things, **wash your hands!** Particularly after cleaning your contaminated filtration pump. And don't stuff midday traveler's snacks into your mouth with grubby paws. I'm a great one for riding third-class buses, running my hands over railings and seat backs and window frames, then at some stop buying a treat from a street vendor—the deliciousness of which is to eat it with my fingers while loitering.

Abide by good advice and you can avoid most cases of traveler's trots, as long as you don't stumble out of the jungle into a colorful roadside café and, delirious, order a bottle of warm pop poured over contaminated ice cubes!

6
For Women Only: How Not to Pee in Your Boots

The significance of my position was
the opportunity for my growth.
—Valerie Fons, *Keep It Moving*

Many a pair of soggy socks, jaundiced sneakers, and rancid leather boots—all mine—attest to the need for this chapter. Men need no pointers on how to pee. Men can pee and maintain the decorum of a three-piece-suiter strolling down Park Avenue. To whizz, men just find a tree. Not to hide behind, thank you, but to lean on while pondering the goings-on of the universe—one hand propped high on the trunk, the other aiming penis. With backs turned, yet in full view, men piss for anyone present, sometimes in baronial silhouette against a blazing sunset, sometimes without a break in the conversation, as if the flaunting of their ritual were the greater part of its pleasure. Women, on the other hand, search for a place to hide (heaven forbid anyone should know we have to pee in the first place) where, with panties dropped and sweet asses bared, we must assume the position of a flustered duck trying to watch itself pass an egg.

Possibly Freud deserves more credit than I normally grant him. Although I don't recall a childhood Oedipal complex, in adulthood there have been occasions when, along with the urge to pee, I've been seized by a fierce penis envy. As a rule, men pee with dignity, it might even be said with class—sometimes with machismo alone, but always with ease. Except when troubled by inclement conditions reflected in the time-honored proverb, "Never into the wind," men, by and large, are carefree pee-ers. It's high time women peed with a similar sense of pride and had as much fun.

So cheer up, my dears, the rest of this chapter is just for us. With a little practice we, too, can cultivate the ultimate in blasé, while being proud of a challenge faced and won, a job well done—not just a piddling vaingloriousness in the operation of an appendage come by genetically!

Had I paid more attention when I was growing up, my grandmother might well have been my illustrious peeing mentor. Now I have only the remembrance of accompanying her into public restrooms. Hoisting her skirts, she would slip one leg out of her wide-legged underdrawers, twist them around the other leg to hold outstretched matador-fashion, and then with the shuffle of a too tightly reined horse, back bowlegged over the bowl and fire away. In those days, I had no time for this bizarre old-fashioned method: I was too busy balancing little bits of folded toilet paper all around the seat (as my mother had taught me), half of which ended upon on the floor from the slight breeze caused by my turning around to sit down. Finding with regularity that a person could water her pants before successfully executing this preparation, I eventually gave it up and just sat down. It was my perhaps ignorant but expedient theory that if everyone else were following this ridiculous paper routine, the seat must surely be free from whatever frightful diseases were to be avoided—diseases never explained, only alluded to mysteriously.

To this day, except where sanitary seat tissues ("butt gaskets" in some circles) are furnished for resting upon, I have yet to master a reliable restroom technique. Sometimes I try bracing myself against the stall's walls, toilet tank, or paper dispenser, or even hanging on to the doorknob (if there is one), in an effort to suspend my bum an inch above the seat. About then I remember a couple of friends: one who lets herself in and out of cubicles and flushes public toilets with her shoe rather than come in skin contact with those germ-ridden levers; the other, a man, who choreographs an elaborate routine for escaping the men's room without touching a thing. Unnerving me further while seated on a sanitary cover is this idle question: If the last person's pee can soak through this thin tissue shield, what else might there be swimming through? Oh, grandmother and baggy underwear, where are you now?

Fortunately, out in the bush we face none of these civilized problems. Give me peeing in the woods any day. Once you get the hang of it, it's a blissful experience. After a long outdoor stint, I find I'm severely depressed with the cold, white, closed-in ambiance and flushing racket of my home bathroom.

In developing countries, another stand-up peeing style (out-shining even my grandmother's) is performed by women who grow up unhampered by pants. The secret lies in the gathering up of a skirt, the tilting of a pelvis and the near bowing of femurs—plus, the sometimes-suggested placement of your first two fingers on either side of the inner labia, to lift and gently position your stream forward—altogether allowing for peeing with Olympian accuracy, and made easier by practice since toddler age. Yet, I recently met a woman in arts and education with the United Nations who fairly boasted she'd learned her stand-up peeing at the age of forty-five, from the Asante women of Ghana.

It's also possible to master a stand-up peeing technique when clothed in a pair of loose-fitting or stretchy shorts, by sliding the crotch material to one side. One friend does this and then squats, but another woman I know can adjust the material and then stand right along a roadside to pee. If, in driving by, you miss seeing her stream, you might guess she was only stretching her legs and soak-ing up the view. Practice is the secret.

Not quite a century ago we were chasing a dress revolution to transport us from skirts and billowing bloomers to trousers like men's. Most women today think of skirts as less than functional in the woods. But really, *anything* goes. "Whatever works" is a good philosophy. Should you so desire, don't hesitate to scramble the outbacks in a dirndl or sarong, as did Robyn Davidson, the author of *Tracks* (New York: Pantheon Books, 1980), when crossing the Australian desert with her camels. When we pass on the trail, I'll recognize another independent, experimental spirit. Someday, who knows, our inhibitions about crotch exposure might evaporate in a rebellion similar to "ban the bra" and bring us full circle to a resurrection of the bare-bottomed leopard-skin mini. For practical purposes! Until then, we have . . .

Purple Rain Adventure Skirt ($71.99) is an above-the-knee design with pockets, a wide and stretchy waist band, *no* attached undershorts, and a choice of colors. Perfect for badasses "going commando!" Or you can layer underneath: with leggings when cold or a bathing suit when heading for a swim in the creek. This small company of outdoor attire (women's skirts and kilts for men, designed by owner and long-distance hiker Mandy Bland) adheres to an amazing regime of leave-no-trace, coupled with environmentally sustainable fabric sourcing and business practices. Mandy walks or bikes packages to the post office. Everything is handmade in her home studio. Inquire about customizing. Now, here's where I tell you that "going commando" not only increases ventilation and reduces moisture, but it also saves on laundry and the cost of undies. Try it, you'll like it. I've done it for years, learned it from my mother.

Purple Rain Adventure Skirts
www.purplerainskirts.com
PO Box 813
Medford, OR 97501
✉ info@purplerainskirts.com

Another simple accessory for outdoor women is a **pee rag**, usually either a full-size or half-bandanna, to use for blotting. Tie it (to dry) on the outside of a backpack and rinse it out whenever you come across water. Or spring for the magical *intentional* product that follows.

Kula Cloth (KC) (½ ounce, $20 to $22) is a beautiful, reusable, antimicrobial, silver-infused pee blotter, developed by Anastasia Allison, former park ranger and police officer, turned, as she says, *adventurepreneur.* Named after Kula Kangri, the tallest mountain in Bhutan, the KC strives to summit peaks of many kinds. While it visually resembles a dainty pot holder, it's made from obsessively researched and highly advanced textiles—one side absorbent, the other waterproof for keeping hands dry—and offered in a growing selection of inspiring designs. KCs are the proud eco-friendly partner of Leave No Trace. You can quit packing excessive amounts of t.p. down the trail. You can—even!—use less t.p. in your home bathroom. A snap-strap attaches it to your pack, and a reflective stripe helps you find it with your headlamp in the dark. Although I'd buy one of these purely in response to Anastasia's passionate story, when it arrived I was stunned to a new level of joy! Visit her website to hear the story of her near-fatal accident, which inspired her assertion to "courageously design your own life."

Kula Cloth
www.kulacloth.com
PO Box 13156
Mill Creek, WA 98208
✉ hello@kulacloth.com

To Sit or to Squat

When wearing jeans, khakis, or tights, and underwear, the process of peeing becomes limited to sitting or squatting (that is, until we get to FUDs later in this chapter). Squatting was never one of my best shots; the liquid soon puddled up and spattered onto everything within three feet. In addition, I'm hereditarily lacking balance genes. With all muscles in tight squatting concentration, my success at relaxing the few correct ones to facilitate peeing without toppling over was comparable to my luck on the slot machines: no jackpots.

Persevering, I began to recognize that after decades of conditioning, I couldn't pee if I couldn't relax, and I couldn't relax if I couldn't sit. So with squatting essentially out of the picture, my experiments narrowed to various approaches to sitting. In my first attempts, I sat on low rocks. This again led to the puddle-up and spatter effect, the only difference being wet thighs instead of wet ankles.

Then came several tries directly on the ground, based on some left-over-from-college-physics notion that proximity decreases velocity—think of pouring lemonade into a pie pan. Direct contact with the earth gave me a thrilling primordial closeness to nature but proved disastrous. Either I ended up sitting in the puddle or, trying a slight incline to avoid that, I wound up with a problem rather like trying to anticipate the flow of Kilauea's lava. How far and in which direction was that steaming stuff going to travel? Usually far enough to engulf the pants draped around my feet. Furthermore, leaves, burrs, twigs, and foxtails—all having a tendency to stick to my buns—would lodge themselves in my undergarments, ending up in more critical cracks and crannies.

A few more days of trial and error dampened yet another theory; sitting on higher objects merely encouraged a more direct route into my boots. But remaining undaunted and enjoying my freedom from walls too much to scurry back to a finely polished, containerized seat, I set off in search of smoother surfaces away from the spray.

As for those of us whose squatting muscles have atrophied (a mutation I'm certain paralleled the advent of privy seats), and for those of us who didn't grow up on the farm or going fishing with grandpa and haven't yet assimilated stand-up peeing are all, nonetheless, wishing to experience a piss in the woods with the same high quality of enjoyment one experiences devouring a piece of good New York cheesecake, here is the secret to **sitting** without peeing in your boots.

First, leave camp in plenty of time to locate an inspiring view and far enough into the bush that your urethra won't tie itself into a bowline at the thought of "being seen." Remember, the *bathroom* acquires its reputation for offering restful respite largely because of its isolation. Now look for a spot with two rocks, or two logs, or a rock and a log close together. Slide your pants down around your ankles and seat yourself near the front edge of one rock. Then prop up your feet—off the ground—on the other. Here you can sit, relax, avoid all showers, and keep sticker free. The steep incline of a hillside, the side of a boulder, or a tree trunk can also be used as the second rock. If you're a bit of a rock climber, you can actually brace yourself in a narrow passageway between two flat-faced boulders or rock walls (a chimney, climbers call it) with your back pressed against one side, your knees bent slightly, and your feet flat against the other.

What's more, if it's masterful coolness you're after, that flaunting of "this is no sweat, I was born a frontierswoman," find a two-rock spot behind a waist-high boulder or bush from where you can casually, with dignity intact, carry on a conversation. Well, maybe not completely intact on the initial try—have patience. The combination of women, peeing, and dignity takes a bit of getting used to—not only for you but also for the people with whom you'll be conversing. Be brave. Act "as if," at first; appear nonchalant. Practice. Teach. Be persistent. Eventually, the world will change. And in the meantime, keep your feet up and dry while gazing blissfully over the misty mountaintops in complete peace and satisfaction.

My advice for **squatting** is to slide undies and pants down *together*, just barely enough not to pee in them. This maneuver will keep you from fighting folds of material that can bunch up behind your knees, or struggling for a solid stance with everything gathered at your ankles, or fully extracting one leg from your attire. Successfully squat and I applaud you!

Navigating Menstruation in the Wild

The other imperative for women traipsing around in the great outdoors is to engineer a discreet, environmental approach to menstruation. You might never feel as sassy as a woman packer I once observed stooped over a campfire cooking breakfast for twenty people. Behind her ear, tucked into her sun-blond curls, where one might stick a pencil, she sported a paper-clad tampon, just waiting for a moment's break in the chores. But for most of us twenty-first-century women of propriety traveling in the company of others (and also for any of us who'd rather not offer opportunity to attribute our natural assertiveness to being "on the rag"—dreadfully, a phrase still in circulation), here are some plans.

Menstrual cups: Washable and reusable, these internally inserted cups provide a strategy that's easy on both pocketbook and environment. For a thorough introduction to the numerous aspects of cups, with intelligent discussion of vaginal shapes and depths; suggestions for cup-folding, insertion, retraction, and cleaning; guidance on finding the right cup size (your, so to speak, "Goldilocks cup"); along with notable brand testing and reviews, visit *Wirecutter:* https://thewirecutter.com/reviews/best-menstrual-cup.

An enthusiastic number of women manage to conquer the learning curve for menstrual cups and fall deeply in love. Others struggle. Getting beyond the item's "ew" factor of its being disturbingly messy is often too much. Cups are best emptied and cleaned at home or in a single-stall bathroom with a sink. Tackling cup maintenance in a busy public restroom is an odds-on shocker, and in the backcountry at least a headache, considering the requirements of water, mild soap, and seclusion. Refreshing a menstrual cup is a decidedly private affair. With camp sanitation always high on my list, followed by not attracting animals and not scaring the beejeezus out of fellow vacationers with scattered seeming grisly crime scenes, I urge the following prudence. Carry a trowel to a location well above any high-water line and bury both blood and soapy water. *Wirecutter*'s article distinguishes between *blood* and *menstrual fluid*, the latter consisting of "blood, vaginal secretions, cervical mucus, and tissue from the endometrium."

Speaking of sanitation, I came near flipping once on a river trip—not in a raft but in aggravation, as the head guide—in stumbling across a woman who'd somehow seen fit to borrow one of our camp chickie pails (used for washing dishes) to launder her underwear and diaphragm. My absence of humor nearly cost me my job. Thankfully, those were the days of campfires; we filled the metal pail with water and *boiled the crap out of it*. In retrospect, probably overkill.

Tampons and sanitary pads: Find a container for storing your major "monthly" supply. I've used a metal Band-Aid box or a lovely antique tin. This size works well for applicator-less tampons. A month's supply fits neatly into the tin, and the tin snugly into the corner of an ammo can, lashed to a raft. When I'm driving a team of horses and my hands stay dirty all day on the trail, I use tampons with applicators. These require a larger container. If you use sanitary pads, you will need one even roomier. The latest designer bag you brought home from boutique shopping, a soft satin travel case, or an old cookie tin will all work. This is the main supply and remains stowed in the depths of your duffel bag or backpack or ammo can.

Next, you need a container for daily use—something to keep handy for slipping items into your pocket when you stroll off in search of your place of easement. A small cosmetic or ditty bag makes for good camouflage, though an ordinary, plastic zip-closing bag will do. Inside, keep the day's supply of whatever you're using, some additional bags for storing refuse (as in, used tampons, sanitary pads, cellophane wrappers, and plastic, all of which must be packed out, not buried, not dropped in portable potties or vault-type outhouses), and lastly a cache of clean t.p. An alternative to t.p. is a pocket packet of tissues that can be doled out quite politely to others in need. During the day, the refuse bags will reside in your day kit, tucked close by in a pocket, fanny pack, saddlebag, ammo can, or outside pocket of a backpack. At evening camp, when you resupply your day kit, you'll transfer the refuse into a larger holding bag in your main supply sack.

Any fecally soiled t.p. must be gathered up, stored, and disposed of separately. It can be burned in a campfire or at home in a woodstove; it can be deposited in your group's portable potty or a trailhead vault-type outhouse, or carefully flushed (in average-size wads) down a toilet connected to a septic or sewer system. For stashing this soiled tissue, opt for a washable, reusable bag—perhaps of water-resistant nylon. (See chapter 4 for handy solo containers for poop-packers.)

On organized expeditions, the central garbage is sometimes sorted into burnable and pack-out refuse. To limit the volume and weight of the pack-out garbage, the paper trash is sometimes burned in the evening campfire or the last thing before breaking camp. Give what you can to the central garbage. (On a private trip, apprise yourself thoroughly of campfire regulations; open fires are not allowed in many areas or may require burn pans and special ash disposal.) Also keep in mind that tampons and sanitary napkins need an inferno of a fire to be immediately and completely consumed. Once, when I was a novice in my newly acquired environmental awareness, I returned to camp under cover of darkness and surreptitiously slipped a small, carefully wadded bundle into the coals. While we sang songs and exchanged flip and wrap stories, to my horror, the fire slowly blackened and peeled away only the wrappings of my gift. The safest approach on a group outing is to ask the trip leader or one of the guides about disposal procedures.

All this attention to garbage is vital. Cock your ear and you'll hear Mother Earth yodeling "THANK YOU!"

The Divine Revolution of FUDs

Now for a word, or a great bunch of words, on transformative feminine funnels, better known as **FUDs** (female urinary devices). These articles to facilitate a woman's peeing come in washable-reusable plastic or silicone or in disposable water-resistant cardboard, and the latter should by rights be available in every public toilet. With slight variations in shape, the principle is basically the same for all models. The funnel, elongated and elliptical, affords a comfortable fit between a woman's legs and allows her to direct her stream. It adds a convenient frontal attack to grandmother's stand-up peeing style, is handy for cramped restrooms (say, in airplanes), yucky-looking toilet seats, landscapes with no cover, and even traffic jams. FUDs are a boon to active women in wheelchairs. Elderly women and pregnant women use them. Marathon runners, pilots, and women in the military love theirs. It was decades ago that I first saw funnels advertised in *Latitude 38*, a sailing and marine publication. They were delighting women sailors who wanted to avoid going below in order to go—a ship's cramped head being the worst spot to hang out if you're prone to seasickness. The funnel entailed no dropping of drawers, only an unzipping of shorts or pulling aside of a bathing suit. Women could stand tall—hip to hip with the men—and pee over the rail. Now FUDs have found homes with women mountain climbers, bicyclists, sea kayakers, skiers, festivalgoers, pub crawlers, big game hunters—even motorcycle mamas. I've met traveling women who've carried theirs on trains, ferries, and buses all over the world. **No more staying dehydrated out of fear of having to pee!**

My initial excitement about funnels was in the thought they might be precisely the solution for sleeping out on nippy nights. With a hose, I might pee at 4:00 a.m. without having to crawl out of my toasty bag. Upon first use, one disadvantage became immediately apparent. The longest of the hoses (and you need the longest in this situation) tends to have a strongly coiled memory. With tenacity, I could stretch it out, but let go and the end could flip around to spray everything in sight like an out-of-control fire hose. In addition, if I expected the liquid to exit the correct end, I had to remember the principle of gravity. Having gone to the trouble of hunting up a perfectly flat spot on which to bed, I had to work hard to stay within the warmth of my bedroll while rising enough to provide a downhill flow. Although I have reports from women who manage this well, I say forget it! A few moments of scampering about in the frost makes me all the more appreciative of a warm bag—just part of the daily allotment of minor inconveniences and miseries that seem to help me retain a healthy and humble perspective on life. Finally, if you're inside a tent with sleet pelting the sides, try coupling a funnel with a collector bag or bottle. For those of us being dragged, kicking and screaming, into the third decade of the twenty-first century, the old coffee can still works fine.

It's for cross-country skiing, to my mind, that the funnel becomes indispensable—when the charming outhouse is a couple miles off and I'm sporting layers of clothing. I'll slip one into a plastic zip bag (though some funnels come with a case) and keep it tucked in an accessible pocket. Then, as proudly as any brother, I can step a dozen feet off the trail and turn my back. With a full bladder, I can even write my name—well, my initials! (But leave no sign, cover that yellow snow.) The funnel has cut my pee forays from sometimes forty-five minutes to three. Previously, I'd been skiing off into the woods, which can actually provide little cover when the ground is a startling white, plowing through knee-deep snow to scout out a spot, then skinning down pants and long johns and trying hopelessly to squat between my skis, a maneuver that would invariably pop my bindings. Digging out was such an exhausting hassle that I often considered lying down and freezing over till spring.

For anyone interested in experimenting with a funnel, the investment is small. And *do* experiment, in the shower or backyard. Spread your legs a bit, bend your knees a little, tuck your pelvis until you can feel a forward lifting of your crotch, and lower the FUD's exit hole to slightly below level—all to help your stream arc outward, *before* downward. (Remember the title of this chapter!) If you have an exceptionally forceful flow, it's possible with some funnels to snip off a bit of the end, like you would the nib of a cake-decorating bag. In action, snug the funnel tight against your body, or give it a little room to breathe in the front—every woman's anatomy is uniquely her own. To avoid a warm, wet surprise, make sure your funnel is fairly well empty before withdrawing it. Use a gentle pressure on the back edge to help in scooping the last drops (perhaps even bypassing the need for t.p.). Urine is sterile as it exits the body unless you have a bladder infection, and this you would know, but your skin in the area is not. Clean your FUD during the day by shaking it vigorously to dry, or rub with a sanitary wipe. When you reach home, wash it with soap and water. Some brands can be boiled and many now boast "dishwasher safe!"

Funnels, in recent years, have blossomed into a bouquet of colorful products, to the extent that you can color-coordinate or make a personal fashion statement. They sell to numerous joyous tunes: "no more tush in the bush," "female freedom," "don't take life sitting down," "stand up and take control," "banish bare bottoms," "pee with ease, save your knees," "because life's greatest adventure shouldn't be finding a restroom." So select your ditty and get weeing.

Washable-Reusable FUDs

The following products are listed in the order of my acquaintance. Visit their wonderful websites for product-specific instructions and videos.

Sports & Travel Freshette Package ($23.95) includes a pink plastic FUD, or olive drab for the military, 5-inch extension tube, and zippered travel pouch. Longer extensions available in 36- and 48-inch lengths, or custom cut. **Collector Bags** ($12.95 for 12-pack) are good for bad-weather tent camping or traffic jams on the way to the woods! Freshette is the world-renowned "original." A buyer's testimonial: "The best thing since the invention of the wheel." I agree.

Freshette
www.freshette.com
International Sani-fem Inc.
PO Box 4117
Downey, CA 90241
✉ sanifem@aol.com
☎ in US: 800-542-5580 (toll-free)
☎ outside US: 562-928-3435

SHEWEE Extreme ($21.80) is a slim funnel of molded plastic, with a 5-inch extension tube and hard plastic carrying case. Choose from eight merry colors. The **Flexi** ($12.11) is a new, larger, flexible funnel and comes with the extension. **Extension tube** (or pipe) by itself ($4.85); a matching **carrying case** ($4.85). The **Peebol** ($9.19 for 3-pack) is a collector bag, useful also for men and children—turns urine into a non-spill gel. Shewee offers a variety of women's underwear with "fly" fronts for funnel access. The **Military Pack** ($38.76) is a Shewee Extreme (all in olive drab), with a pair of black T-Fronts (fitted underwear with a discreet fly front). See website for shipping from various distributors.

SHEWEE
www.shewee.com
Shewee Ltd.
New Road (A65)
Ingleton, Via Carnforth
North Yorkshire, LA6 3HL UK
✉ info@shewee.com
☎ 015242 41477

GoGirl funnel ($12.99 with carrying tube; $18.99 with 12-inch extension tube) is made of flexible, medical-grade silicone (can withstand boiling) and has a built-in splash guard. Available in lavender or khaki. Comes rolled up in a carrying tube with a tissue and baggie. GoGirl is a primarily female-operated, t.p.-less, solar-powered business.

GoGirl
www.go-girl.com
FemMed Inc.
1191 Northland Drive
Mendota Heights, MN 55120
✉ customerservice@go-girl.com
☎ 877-447-5007

Pibella Travel ($19) is a slim, Swiss-made funnel of unique design made of polypropylene. The "small and feminine docking orifice" (4.0 × 1.6 cm) fits just over the urethra exit, between the labium. Comes in pink, green, or pearl, with a dark blue plastic zip bag. Wash by rinsing, sterilize by boiling. Also dishwasher safe. Sold in many outdoor stores (see website for locations) or off the internet, with free shipping worldwide. Selected as "Best" in *Backpacker* magazine's 2015 complete guide to FUDs. "Highly appreciated by teens and grandmas alike!" The **Pibella Comfort** ($49.00; urination tube with lid, and 3 urine bags) is a little different in shape for use in a wheelchair.

Pibella
www.pibella.com
Pibella GmbH
Heimentalstrasse 53
5430 Wettingen, Switzerland
✉ contact@pibella.com

pStyle ($12) has its own distinctive design, a sort of waterslide. Made of rigid plastic that easily sheds water and comes in seven fun colors. Press this one firmly against your body. Because it's not fashioned as a tube but open along the top, it breathes on its own. When finished, "pull the rounded back edge forward with a bit of upward pressure" to catch the last drips. Reportedly works well for women climbers while in harness. Although the principal users of pStyles are women, the company's philosophical core promotes an intersectional and inclusive ethic, with easy peeing for all. The **pCase** ($12) is a handmade case of organic cotton with Velcro closing. See the website for bulk sales and retail locations.

pStyle
www.thepstyle.com
PO Box 31
Dowelltown, TN 37059-0031
✉ contact@thepstyle.com
☎ 615-241-0014

Disposable FUDS

Do not flush disposables, discard them in the trash.

Uri-Mate Protector ($9.95 for 5-pack, 3 cones to a pack) is a biodegradable, thin cardboard cone. Comes in a cellophane packet, a smidgeon larger and flatter than a teabag, with a sweet pink rose graphic. Just unfold. Instructions in English and Spanish. Available online from distributors in the UK, US, and Venezuela.

Uri-Mate Protector
www.uri-mate.com
Uri-Mate Head Office
32 Hartley Road
London, E11 3BL, UK
✉ info@uri-mate.com
☎ 786-317-6254

P-MATE ($4.95 for 5-pack) is a single-use "stand-to-pee device" of form-fashioned cardboard with a thin wax coating. Flat-folded, it literally pops open. Comes in colorful designs. Available online from distributors in various countries.

P-MATE
www.pmateusa.com
PO Box 1854
Broomfield, CO 80038
✉ info@pmateusa.com
☎ 720-317-3303

GoGirl Stand Up also offered by GoGirl ($6.99 for 3-pack) is a disposable, single-use option. The Stand Up is hot pink and biodegradable. Unfold and squeeze open to use. Contact information on page 93.

In closing this chapter, to warm your hearts, I pass along the following story related to me years ago by an employee of a Sausalito, California, yachting supply house:

> *After carefully selecting a pink plastic funnel, an elderly white-haired couple arrived at the cash register, whereupon the woman demurely inquired whether a longer hose might be attached for her. Her request was gladly granted and the funnel whisked away to the back workroom. Then, lifting her gentle, wisdom-aged face toward her husband, with a cherubic wink she crooned, "Now, dear, mine will be longer than yours!"*

7

What? No T.P.? Or Doing Without

Back to the Pleistocene

—An Earth First! bumper sticker

Conjure up for a moment one of those predawn mornings when you emerge reluctantly from the warm bedding and bump along the walls to the bathroom, to sit, just another shadow, hunched on the bowl. Eyes shut against the real world, elbows dug into knees, and chin settled in a cradle of knuckles, you are soon drowsily appreciating the serenity following a particularly portly poop. Then, wishing you could beam yourself back to horizontal again, you blindly grope for the toilet paper only to find your fingertips spinning a naked cylinder of cardboard, sending up the flapping racket of a pinwheel. Rats! You're forced to flip on all one hundred watts, stumble across the room to the cabinet under the sink, fish out and unwrap a new roll. You might exchange it for the empty one (if you were truly a good person), but the dexterity involved would require your final emergence from dreamland.

Or how about this: It's one of those ghastly, highfalutin dinner parties—not casual, not just old friends. It could be a Waterford and Limoges setting at the elderly boss's estate or maybe the new girlfriend's esteemed literary family all gathered to look you over. The seven-course meal has been consumed, yet the formality of intercourse has not relaxed. As a matter of fact, the guests are perched around the ornate living room like so many stately, stoic great blue herons, quietly picking at thinly-layered desserts and sipping cognac. Suddenly, amid all this propriety, the spiced prune conserve that accompanied the main course, but which now is somewhere south of your stomach, screams at you to leap up and excuse yourself—politely, of course, on the pretense of helping (the kitchen staff?) with the dishes.

Once into the hallway, with downward-pointed toes lifted high in double time—a perfect rendition of Sylvester the Cat—you detour to the powder room. Shortly thereafter comes the discovery that your hostess has neglected to renew the supply of toilet paper, which—unbeknownst to you—she keeps in the hall closet. You've finished crawling through all the cupboards: Now what? Do you hobble to the door with your pants around your knees, poke your nose through the crack, and utter *psst?* Whenever someone disappears into the bathroom at a party, others will imagine them preening before the mirror, checking for spinach between the teeth, "freshening up," or—possibly—tinkling. Straining and pooping? Never. All pretenses go out the window when you must holler for toilet paper (in a pinch, even a woman will drip-dry Number One). For the rest of the evening, you might as well be wearing a sandwich board bearing three-foot headlines of what you were up to.

Next is the classic Gas Station Mad Dash: surely there isn't a person in the First World who's escaped this one. It begins with the feverish circling of the facility in an effort to park nearest the doors with the stick-figure emblems. Either one that's empty is fair game in emergencies. Somehow you manage to climb out of your vehicle, dance across the pavement doing a doubled-over cowboy schottische (inspired by a constricted sphincter muscle), and throw open the restroom door—oh, miracle of miracles!—without having to humiliate yourself by begging for a key. But there your good fortune ends. Almost immediately you realize the only scraps of toilet paper are flotsam on the lake in which you're standing, there isn't a shred of tissue in any of your pockets, and the paper towel dispenser is "Jeez, why me?" empty.

For pure perspective, I'll recount the above stories, or equally painful paperless scenarios, when people respond to the idea of experimenting in the woods without t.p. as though they'd fallen into a vat of putrefying fish guts. There's nothing so disgusting about it, really.

As with all major changes, adjusting to the absence of our readily available soft quilted white stuff wound neatly 'round a cylinder takes a bit of getting used to. Once successfully maneuvered, however, scrubbing one's posterior with a snatch of biodegradable nature is a noteworthy experience, whereupon one's ecologically prescribed place in the universe may come vividly into focus. Puffed up with pride, or jubilant with primitive freedom, one might be startled to hear a rousing chorus of approval from the forest fairies. So I've been told.

Doing without toilet paper takes me back, way back. Old Mr. Neanderthal might well have enjoyed skin like horsehide and not needing to wipe. I swear I can sense ghostly forms—him and his buddies?—lurking about, curious, every time I walk away from a purely organic burial of shit and leaves. After an accomplishment of this sort, I'll bounce along absurdly pleased with myself, a euphoric little note within a great harmony. Such mysterious brushes with my deepest origins not only overwhelm but also refresh me, as tangibly as a hot shower after a week of mountain sweat and dirt. All at once I feel powerfully attached to a cosmic whole, simple in an age of complexity, perfectly in tune with the world, yet tiny and humble, and, of all things, enchantingly ancient. Vats of putrefying fish guts—phooey!

Be it a personal quest to function as simply as the primeval wandering tribes, or a feeling of bliss at not having to pack around rolls of bulky tissue and bags of carry-out garbage—whatever your motivation, here are a few suggestions to get you started. The library is not full of pertinent references to t.p. alternatives, and I will never have covered enough ground to have all the answers. You'll have to depart from the text after finishing this chapter and experiment on your own. Call it scientific research.

Leaves, Stones, Pinecones, and All

When I began my evaluation of leaves, I remembered my dear high school friend Jan who once traveled across Europe keeping a toilet paper diary, replete with sample bits from different countries. She returned to the States with everything from pieces of brown wrapping paper to wax paper and shrink-wrap. Is it, I wonder, worth speculating on the regional correlations between indigenous plant leaves and present-day toilet paper quality? If you think you have trouble selecting brands in the supermarket, wait until you see the spectrum nature has to offer.

A vast assortment, some obviously more appropriate to the task than others, are yours for the picking. But wait. A few words of caution are necessary.

> There are many wildland items suitable for natural toilet paper, and the choice of living plants should be only a last resort. If you pick leaves at all, be especially mindful. Always select dead grasses and leaves over live ones. Don't pick wildflowers or rare species. Don't pick in parks or other restricted areas. Don't pull anything up by the roots. Don't rob large clumps or strip entire branches. Carefully pick a leaf here, a leaf there—so no one, not even the plant (especially the plant), will know you have been there. In the following pages you will find many suggestions for nonliving t.p. substitutes.

To hunt leaves, an introductory course in botany is not necessary; neither must you learn every leaf by name. But engrave in your memory poison oak, poison ivy, poison sumac, and those sneaky stinging nettles, all illustrated in any good field guide. A dinner date with Frankenstein's monster or the Wicked Witch of the West would be a joyous interlude compared to the aftermath of using one of those leafy devils on your keister. Should you be serious in planning to hang out with my Neanderthaloid apparitions and also be a member of the species I call "Exotic Trekkies" (those who roam about in out-of-the-way climes), then read up on the vegetation native to the areas you plan to visit, to ascertain whether some peculiar variety of poison pine or viperous honeysuckle should be added to your don't-touch list.

When leaf-stalking, look for the large and the soft. Mullein leaves are a favorite: soft, cushy, almost woolly, and one leaf will do. Thimbleberry is another large-leafed plant and praiseworthy once you discover the soft side opposite the slick. Plants with small or palmated leaves can be used by the handful (remember—one here, one there). Frequently, there will be no perfect specimen available. At those times, the profusion and ample diameters of leaves such as California's wild grape can offer compensation for their waxy slickness.

Before picking, be sure to examine leaves carefully; they sometimes can be sticky (as though covered by a thin layer of syrup), scabrous (having a rasplike surface), annoyingly prickly owing to small bristles and barbs or, more seriously, *hispidulous* (covered with sharp hairs stiff enough to penetrate the skin). Stay away from reeds, bamboo, and some grasses—in effect, slicing leaves—that can cause agonizing wounds like paper cuts. With a little attention, you'll learn which ones to avoid and be on your way to becoming a connoisseur of fine leaves.

Autumn woodlands—not to be shamed by the swankiest powder room décor—offer us a leaf selection in vibrant designer shades. Not all fallen leaves dry and crumble immediately. In some climates, many will stay pliable through the winter months. Alpine winters, where deciduous vegetation is scarce, can be a bit of a problem. For a matter of months in many parts of the high country, evergreens are the only selection. Draw on your creativity. Dried pine needles can be put to good use, provided you have the time to line them all up in the same direction. The odd stick on the ground might be useful, if it's smooth and you remember to rub with the grain. Foresters of the Northwest are partial to something I've always known to make great Halloween handlebar mustaches—the dark brown *Bryoria* lichen that hangs abundantly from trees in long gauzy streamers. There's also the yellowish green *Alectoria*. And pinecones are reputedly good tools, but avoid the spiky rotund cones, stick with the narrow, softer, aging species. A world-renowned river rafter of my acquaintance swears by old spongy Douglas fir cones. Try sheets of smooth peeling bark, polished driftwood, seashells, and large feathers. Steer clear of mosses; they're fragile, shouldn't be disturbed, and crumble uselessly anyway.

In the rural areas of many countries, there are people who've never laid eyes on toilet paper. In parts of the Middle East, a person carries a wet cloth into the fields. The custom of religiously eating with the right hand was not born of divine Arab vision but of prudent hygiene: the left hand-wiped. I wouldn't want to discourage you if this particular system works for you, but before settling on it permanently, you might consider that for journeys longer than a day, you're going to be plagued by an accumulation of feculent cloths to wash, at home or well away from any watercourse.

My cross-country skiing partner promotes snowballs as the perfect winter wipe—that is, once you brace yourself for a momentary shock. Try it. Mold one end to a point. To me, the gentle freeze is a minor trauma compared to, say, visiting one of those inglorious chemical toilets that sit, invariably in the sun, on construction sites and at festivals, exuding gagging aromas from the contents cooking within. Yuk!

Have you ever found yourself with nary a leaf or splash of water to save your life? Arid, sandy terrains are the most critically lacking in t.p. substitutes. In a dry creek bed you can sometimes find a smooth, sun-baked stone—state-of-the-art wipe! But beware. Under a blazing sun, stones can gather enough BTUs to brand cattle. Before using a stone, test it in your hand, then on your wrist as you would the milk in a baby's bottle. And remember not to return a poopy stone to the creek bed.

The Water Wipe

There exists another paperless technique, but it seldom emerges as an option with our persnickety Western ways, which seem by cultural edict to require keeping copious wads between our fingertips and our bums. This approach comes to us mostly by way of Old World countries and from one well-traveled family physician, Dr. Charles Helm, who was born in South Africa and made his way to remote northern British Columbia to set up his practice. We'll call his technique the "water wipe."

Nothing is needed but a container for water: a canteen, bottle, cup, cook pot, and hat have all been suggested. Fill your container and carry it to your chosen spot. Then, squatting over your one-sit hole, trickle water from the container into your free hand—never contaminating the fresh water—and use it to splash or wipe. This trickling procedure poses no problem for agile squatters, but, having been born minus a balance gene, I find it a difficult maneuver. Almost as efficient as trickling is the repeated moistening of one hand, customarily the left.

The water wipe has definite pluses. For the minimalist, it saves on space and weight—both carry-in and carry-out—and it saves trees (soiled t.p. is not recycled). Unless you're in terrain short on water, the water wipe becomes the ideal wipe. (Tissue can still be carried for instances of trekker's trots.) Don't forget to wash your hands.

Then Dr. Helm takes the whole matter to yet another level, saying that if we were to model our diets more after that of horses, we might dispense altogether with wiping, being able ourselves to "neatly pinch off" road apples. A healthy human, Helm believes, need not carry *bogroll* (*bog* is a South African euphemism for bathroom) into the wilderness. Though he admits "the fastidious and prudish amongst our number will not be impressed with a blanket ban on bogroll in the bush."

In a long letter, he holds forth:

> Have you ever watched a horse shit? . . . the process begins with a fart by way of preamble, followed by a voluntary relaxation of the anal sphincter, the passage of a number of well-formed, not-too-hard, not-too-soft turds, then a gentle, well-coordinated contraction . . . [whence the whole] falls to the ground without any of its substance remaining adhered to the horse. The entire process is easy, efficient, and above all has no need of toilet paper.

> Our Western diets have wreaked havoc with our bowel regularity, leading to stools of varying consistency and a consequent increased need for bogroll. We have not only lost the art of shitting in the woods, we have lost the art of shitting, period. Perhaps it is related to the innate fear of being caught with a turd half-in and half-out, but your average mortal will constrict that sphincter as soon as a respectable fraction has seen the light of day. No turd can withstand this kind of strangulation, and inevitably the distal portion

*breaks off, the proximal part remains put, and a sub-
stantial segment close to the sphincter gets smeared
all over. I suspect that most humans tighten that dread
sphincter half a dozen times per crap. And the bogroll
industry gloats and smirks.*

There's definitely something to be said in this regard for a meatless, high-fiber diet.

There you have it: all I know today.

Hmmm? Well, I did once meet a man who proposed I curry my bum with sand in the mountain man's age-old manner of scouring pots and pans. But I have a hunch this curmudgeonly old bugger was—or had, like my own Mr. N.—a horse-hide's ass. Me, I'll stick to snowballs and stones.

Now you're on your own.

Acknowledgments

A quick glance over my shoulder at this guide's thirty-one years and four editions reveals a red carpet of gratitude lengthier now than the chapters. For the current champions and contributors, as well as original players and those who've bestowed balanced and thoughtful and kindly oomph, my unbound thanks goes out to the following people and parties:

The late Jon Runnestrand for never failing to affirm my choice of untrodden paths, urging me—above all else—to "God damn it, keep rowing!" Don't chuck the oars in a rash leap for safety atop a mid-river boulder.

Mark DuBois and Marty McDonnell, who, eons ago, gently straightened out my urban ways, presenting me with a healthy dose of respect for Mother Nature and offering clues to the real and simple joys in life. Mark, in addition, for his many contributions and careful editing of the first edition, other editions, and a sweetly enduring friendship. Craig Reisner for heightening my sensitivities to the human impact, and Rick Spittler for hours of environmental brainstorming. Howard Backer, MD, for editing the *Giardia* section in the first edition and supplying further updates.

Bill McKibben—favorite author, climate activist, crisis warrior—for penning the Foreword to this edition. I'm over-the-top grateful and positively tickled. Onward we go, in solidarity.

My first woman friend, my precious liberated mother, for believing in me and in this book upon its first publication when she was ninety years old.

My treasure of sisters who blow bubbles into the air or offer life rafts, whatever's needed through the highs of laughable nutziness and lows of toughest turmoil: Carol Newman, Joanne Solberg, Carolee Wilson, Alexis Raleigh, Joyce Ciemny, Barbara Ellis, Lizzie Young, Martha Massey, Linda Cunningham . . . and deeply missed Katya Merrell, Jan Reiter, and Susan Adams.

Suzanne Lipsett, who remains forever in my heart as an ace friend and editor.

T. Mike Walker, my one creative writing teacher, which came about only as a result of my "flunking" the English upper division entrance exam at (then) San Francisco State—and without whose praise, recalled years later, this guidebook might have never been attempted.

Phil Wood, genius publisher, fondly remembered in his wild Hawaiian prints.

My agent and cherished friend Robert Stricker, for beating down my door and making everything happen and happen and happen.

The amazing full-tilt-boogie Ten Speed team for their talent, insight, deft hands, support in tedious matters, and endless good humor: Kimmy Tejasindhu, master-juggler and graceful, exacting editor; Abhimanyu Sandal, designer extraordinaire; Sarah Weitzman, cover artist divine; Jean Blomquist, super-duper copyeditor; Dan Myers, expert production manager; and ever-steady Julie Bennett.

Countless others who've offered encouragement, direction, inspiration, life support, or comradery. To name but a few: Connie Thomas, Bruce Raley, Bob Volpert, Herb Schilling, Joan Hintz, Frank and Ronita Egger, Glenn and Dottie Johnshoy, Mel Mooers, Michael Helling, Bill LaCroix, Amy Sage, Daniel Webb, Marshall Newman, Michael Fahey, Jeannie Warner, Tina St. John, Andrew Clark, Fredi Bloom, and the very funny Kristine Route.

The Indiana and Soo family: Bill and Sandy Robbins.

The Earth family: Sash, Marina, Chris, Ken, Roger, Mary, Gay, Sandy, April, Mike, Kathy, Veronica, Don, Deb, hot-rocks-Leonard, Jed and Michelle and Cousin Pete, Tom, Woody, the holy women and grandfathers . . . from whom I derive strength and heart and health, and share astounding potlucks.

In celebration of life: Jim Hansen, Georgia Milan, Laura Shelton, David Bellamah, Patrick Danaher, David Allmacher, Tim Nielsen, Amy Messer, Larry Stayner, Sherry Peach, and Dean Chow. And then sooo many—can I remember?—at St. Mary's Hospital: Jun, Faith, Isabel, Romeo, Georgette, Noel, Natalie, Twisha, Dana, Althea, Al, Susan, Grace, Jese, Eric, Nelson, Janet, Maru, Ilene, Helen, Marc Wakasa, and Benjamin Maeck. And the two pilots who lifted me off planes.

Phil, Nick, and Dexter—could never, ever have done it without you.

All the helpful people at the Environmental Protection Agency (prior to 2017), Centers for Disease Control and Prevention, US

Forest Service, Bureau of Land Management, National Park Service, Colorado Outward Bound, National Outdoor Leadership School, Leave No Trace Center for Outdoor Ethics, numerous sanitary districts, libraries, and outdoor stores. Brian Oram at Wilkes University Center for Environmental Quality, Environmental Engineering, and Earth Sciences; David Rootes, director of Antarctic Logistics and Expeditions; and Roger Robinson, Chief Mountaineering Ranger at Denali National Park and Preserve.

Bob Abbott and LuVerne Grussing—original cornerstones.

The many who have written or emailed (there's been no shortage of eagerness to comment on this subject), adding significant depth to these chapters. All those mentioned within these pages and those not but deserving of my utter indebtedness for so unabashedly sharing a worst-shit story, knowing full well it would be spread before the world. You know who you are. What else can I say!

My beloved Patricio, always the sweep boat: to you my unbridled love and gratitude, this time for catering to my every need, appointment, and craving, as well as attending to all the chores, the winter wood and broken plumbing, while I wrote much of this edition from bed.

Afterword

We need to foster a bosom friendship with land and water and air. I did not once write the word wilderness in these pages without some cringing and self-evaluation, and remembering the telling words of Chief Luther Standing Bear of the Oglala Sioux:

> We did not think of the great open plains, the beautiful rolling hills, and winding streams with tangled growth, as "wild." Only to the white man was nature a "wilderness" and only to him was the land "infested" with "wild" animals and "savage" people. To us it was tame. Earth was bountiful and we were surrounded with the blessings of the Great Mystery. Not until the hairy man from the east came and with brutal frenzy heaped injustices upon us and the families we loved was it "wild" for us. When the very animals of the forest began fleeing from his approach, then it was that for us the "Wild West" began.

For this fourth edition, in these times of planetary crisis, I offer the prayerful words of Art Solomon, an Anishinaabe Elder, from his poem "Grandfather Story":

> Grandfather,
> Look at our brokenness. . . .
>
> Teach us love, compassion, and honour
> That we may heal the earth
> And heal each other.

Definition of Shit

¹**shit** \'shĭt\ *vb* **shit** also **shat** \'shăt\; **shit-ting/-s** [alter. (Influenced by ²shit and the past and past part. forms) of earlier *shite*, fr. ME *shiten*, fr. OE *scītan*; akin to MLG & MD *schīten* to defecate, OHG *scīzan*, MHG *schīzan*, ON *skīta* to defecate, OE *scēadon* to divide or separate—more at SHED] *vi* **1 a:** to defecate **b:** used *figuratively* to express embarrassment <I thought I'd ~ when I had to pee and there wasn't any place to hide.> **c:** also *figuratively* to express fear <I just about ~ when I stepped off the ski lift and viewed the hill from above.> ~ *vt* **1:** to defecate something <~ watery stools> **2:** to fool, to mislead, to put on <You wouldn't ~ me about using pinecones for t.p., would you?>.

shit 2x4s; *usually* preceded by *eat sawdust and* ~ **1:** to overwork someone **2:** to work full-hearted, or like a demon **3:** also indicating someone who's extremely accomplished <Watch her drive those nails! She can *eat sawdust and* ~ !>.

shit bricks; **1:** to worry in the extreme **2:** to be terrified.

shit can; **1:** to throw away **2:** to ban **3:** to fire or dismiss.

shit fruit salad (also: *shit nickels, shit ice cream*); said of a prima donna <She's so special, she must ~.>.

shit hammer; to assemble by brute force without much thinking.

shit in the woods; **1:** rhetorical reply to a statement of the obvious when preceded by *Does a bear* ~. **2:** a superb outdoor guide when preceded by *How to* ~.

shit on; **1:** to ruin, to muck up. **2:** to treat unfairly; *often* by being extremely rude or unkind or harsh.

shit oneself; **1:** to defile oneself with excrement. **2:** to deceive oneself <He's ~*ing himself* about hiking thirty miles before lunch.>.

shit reverse; to unshit a situation and make it good again.

shit the bed; **1 a:** to foul your nest **b:** to stupidly mess up your own good situation. **2:** to die.

²**shit** \'shĭt\ *n* **-s** [fr. (assumed) ME, fr. OE *scite* (attested only in place names); akin to MD *schit, schitte* excrement, OE *scītan* to defecate] **1 a:** excrement, feces, poop **b:** a case of diarrhea, *used* in plural and preceded by *the*; also a dreary or rotten situation <Camping in this cold, damp cave with ghosts is *the* ~.> **2 a:** garbage; junk <Never leave ~ in the woods.> **b:** unorganized or unrelated articles, stuff **3:** lies, nonsense, exaggeration <a bunch of ~> **4:** something of little value <not worth a ~> **5:** nothing, *usually* in negative construction <We didn't know ~ about poop-packing.>

6: an exclamation (emphatic form) of annoyance, *pronounced* \shē-'it\<Well, ~ ! I peed my pants.>.

a shit; derogatory term indicating a person with mean or bad behavior <She leaves her dog's poop in the middle of the trail. What a ~ !>.

bad shit; a consumable of piss-poor quality; *gen.* refers to street drugs.

big shit; someone with an overinflated sense of self-importance.

blow (a person's) shit away; **1:** to kill **2:** *figuratively*, to astound.

built like a brick shit house; to be solidly or massively built.

bullshit; **1 a:** lies **b:** nonsense **2:** trash; useless junk **3:** name of a group word game **4 a:** an interjection of fierce disagreement **b:** angry retort.

chickenshit; **1:** a coward **2:** petty behavior. *~adj.* cowardly <What a ~ idiot, leaving behind a Wag Bag.>.

crock of shit; something false or deceptive <Campaign promises are a ~.>.

dipshit; an idiot, nerd.

dish out shit; **1:** to deliver reprimands or punishment.

doesn't know shit from Shinola; can't tell the difference between excrement and brown shoe polish.

dogshit; **1:** low-down, dirty, trashed-out **2:** *interjection* expressing hot disapproval.

Don't give me that shit!; **1:** shut up **2:** don't kid me.

dumbshit; a pathetic incompetent.

eat shit; **1:** to lose a game by a large margin **2:** to get a very raw deal **3:** to withstand verbal insults, even physical abuse **4:** to humble oneself **5:** an angry exclamation, meaning get lost, or drop dead.

get your shit together; **1:** undergo great personal growth; to become organized or focused **2:** admonition to hurry up.

good shit; a product of excellent quality or flavor; *gen.* a reference to street drugs.

Holy shit!; exclamation of surprise, discovery, realization, or fear.

horseshit; **1:** lies, double-talk **2:** *interjection* of vehement disagreement.

hot shit; **1:** a class act; *freq.* used sarcastically <Just because she rowed her dinghy through a hurricane, she thinks she's ~.> **2:** a popular item.

jack shit; a negative value; to do ~ is to do less than nothing.

know your shit; to be an expert in your field.

little shit; **1:** person of small stature **2:** term of endearment for someone who is looked upon as a sweet rascal.

Mickey Mouse bullshit; annoying or unimportant issues.

No shit!; **1:** an exclamation ranging from high excitement to surprise; often similar to *Really?* **2:** an expression of sarcasm in response to something already known **3:** an exclamation of hearty agreement.

Oh, shit!; **1:** when *pronounced* \ō 'shĭt\ an exclamation of surprise or disgust; a warning of impending doom; also can mean *Whoops!*; **2:** when *pronounced* \ō 'shē-it\ indicates great pain or embarrassment, or a colossal disaster; **3:** when *pronounced* \aw shĭt\ expresses regret or sympathy or shyness.

old shit; things or ideas that have become outmoded; behavior patterns that no longer work; old baggage or agendas.

piece of shit; **1:** cheaply constructed article **2:** bad or worthless person.

scare the living shit out of; terrorize.

shitcan; toilet; honey bucket; garbage can.

shit happens; expresses the sentiment "the best-laid plans often go awry"; often seen on bumper stickers.

shit hits the fan; **1:** violent or unpleasant situation, often in reference to reprimands coming down from authority figures **2:** major organizational shake-up.

Shit, man!; *pronounced* \sheet män\ **1:** generic expression for surprise, disgust, or anger **2:** expression of delight, pleasure, appreciation, or astonishment.

shit on a brick; exclamation of great disgust <Well, ~>.

shit on a shingle; institutional serving of creamed chipped beef on toast.

shit on wheels; **1:** someone who gets a lot done **2:** a holy terror **3:** a braggart who nevertheless carries it off.

shit or get off the pot; quit wasting time or stalling; make a decision.

shit out of luck; having ill fortune.

shoot the shit; to engage in friendly conversation; *as in* the title of Kathleen's blog, "Shooting the Shit."

stay out of my shit; admonition to mind your own business; to stop meddling.

sure as shit; a very definite and *sometimes* predictable occurrence; true to form.

take a shit; to defecate.

take shit; to accept abuse or ridicule.

tough shit; **1:** expression indicating bad luck, *similar* to *Too bad!* or *That's the way the cookie crumbles!* **2:** angry retort, stronger than *So what!*

up shit creek; in a bad situation <~ *without a paddle*>.

shitaree \'shĭt-a-'rē\ *n.* a toilet, portable potty, something one shits into.

shit-ass *n.* a reprehensible individual.

shit-bird *n.* a mild, *sometimes* half-affectionate name for a scoundrel.

shit-brain *n.* an idiot.

shit burgers *interj.* mild exclamation of dismay or disappointment.

shit disturber *n.* an instigator.

shit-eating; *adj.* used with *grin*; a smile of overt satisfaction.

shit-faced *adj.* drunk or otherwise intoxicated.

shit-fire *n.* **1:** a mean, nasty person; a bully **2:** a bold, often sexually hot, expert at something.

shit-fit *n.* a temper tantrum; a violent tizzy.

shit-head *n.* halfway between a shit-ass and a shit-bird.

shit-hole *n.* **1 a:** a toilet **b:** the hole in the privy board; *often* used *figuratively* <Inventing real biodegradable bags for packing-it-out would not be throwing money down the ~> **2:** the anus **3:** an undesirable place. *~adj.* (spelled shithole) rotten, despicable <He's a ~ hunter, shooting that deer from his truck window.>.

shit-house *n.* **1:** bathroom or outhouse; **2:** indicating someone in disrepute <Oh boy, she's in the ~ now.>.

shit-house poet *n.* **1 a:** anyone who scribbles graffiti on restroom walls **b:** a lousy poet.

shitless *adj.* state of extreme fear <scared ~>.

shit list *n.* a figurative list for persons held in rotten esteem <Whoever forgot the toilet paper is definitely on the ~.>.

shit load *n.* **1:** big, huge, behemoth **2:** reference to something deceitful <What a ~ of crap!>.

shit-put *n.* the act of jumping in saltwater for an overboard defecation from a sea kayak; also called an *aqua dump*.

shit shark *n.* person who operates a honey wagon.

shit storm *n.* **1:** fiery response, *as in* emotional eruption **2:** an actual barrage of weaponry or extreme weather.

shitter \shĭtər\ *n.* **1 a:** outhouse; toilet; bathroom; restroom **b:** used with *time*; a place to think things out; discipline in a drug rehab program.

shitty \'shĭt-ē\ *adj.* **shit-ti-er, -est 1:** inept **2:** inferior quality, cheap, bad, or ugly <These are ~ hiking boots.> **3:** denotes a state of being that is somehow dreadful, *sometimes* as a result of agonizing pain or guilt <My pee ran right into that little mole's hole and now I'm feeling ~.>.